James Robert Page

The pretensions of Bishop Colenso to impeach the wisdom and veracity of the compilers of the Holy Scriptures considered

James Robert Page

The pretensions of Bishop Colenso to impeach the wisdom and veracity of the compilers of the Holy Scriptures considered

ISBN/EAN: 9783337284206

Printed in Europe, USA, Canada, Australia, Japan

Cover: Foto ©Lupo / pixelio.de

More available books at **www.hansebooks.com**

THE PRETENSIONS

OF

BISHOP COLENSO

TO

IMPEACH THE WISDOM AND VERACITY

OF THE

Compilers of the Holy Scriptures

CONSIDERED.

BY THE

REV. JAMES R. PAGE, M.A.

EDITOR OF
"Burnet's Exposition of the Thirty-nine Articles:"
AUTHOR OF
"Position of the Church of England in the Catholic World,"
&c. &c. &c.
AND FORMERLY DEPUTY CHAPLAIN OF THE CHAPEL ROYAL, HAMPTON COURT.

"For had ye believed Moses, ye would have believed Me: for he wrote of Me. But if ye believe not his writings, how shall ye believe My words?"
JOHN v. 46, 47.

LONDON:
RIVINGTONS, WATERLOO PLACE.
1863.

LONDON:
GILBERT AND RIVINGTON, PRINTERS,
ST. JOHN'S SQUARE.

PREFACE.

Bishop Colenso must not be surprised or offended if I have spoken of his book in plain language. There is not, however, any thing farther from my mind than to offer him the least possible personal offence. I have claimed the same mere right to speak of his work which he has claimed, and used, in speaking of the writings of Moses. In a few places I have treated the arguments of the Bishop with irony; which some may think might have been omitted. But when I came to consider, on the one hand, the great object which the Bishop had in view, viz. to overthrow the testimony of Moses; and then, on the other hand, the most laughable arguments by which he sought to accomplish his object; memory, which, like conscience, is sometimes a most inconvenient friend, brought up the love of wit, of which, with Horace, I thought that the flying years had robbed my mind.

By Bishop Colenso's own testimony (pp. vi. vii. of his Preface) he was a kind of unbeliever before he accepted the office of a Bishop.

But he quieted his scruples by some specious explanations. When the Bishop took "Holy Orders," he must have known what the Church requires of her clergy, before she sends them forth to "feed the Church of God, which He hath purchased with His own blood." To have taken Holy Orders under such circumstances was very strange conduct; but to have gone further, and have taken the high office and emoluments of a Bishop, was not, to say the least, consistent with that respect which every man owes to himself, as well as to society. Such conduct has too much the appearance of a man voluntarily branding himself with the curse on the race of Eli,—" Put me, I pray thee, into one of the priest's offices, that I may eat a morsel of bread."

In no other way has the Church been more injured than by such practice. The manner in which too many young men are set apart for the sacred ministry, because they have interest with patrons, or because there are family livings in reserve for them; and without any serious consideration on the part of friends, patrons, or the youth himself, of the great end for which the Church has been planted in the land,—has done more to injure the Church, and to spread infidelity, than all the attacks of its worst enemies could have accomplished. And while such policy and such scandal continue, bishops, clergy, and laity may devise one scheme after another for the regeneration of the people,—but all will be in vain. Any good done, will be done because the Providence of Almighty God overrules all things for His own purposes. But the ministrations of the Church will be void of that life and power necessary to awaken a world by nature " dead in trespasses and sins." But it is not my province to set up as a reformer of the Church.

The Preface of Bishop Colenso does not call for much notice in addition to that bestowed on it in the several parts of my work. The public, for instance, has not any thing to do with his friendship, his feelings, and his experience; nor with his sympathy with — in his own phraseology —" brave souls that yearn for light, and battle for the truth," as if the light of the Revelation of God were darkness. Nor have we much to do with his "sorrow-stricken souls which require support" from his principles, because the amazingly gracious words of Him who said—" Let not your heart be troubled;"—" In the world ye shall have tribulation; but in Me ye shall have peace;"— were mere delusion, and mockery of the afflicted race of man!

Neither need we concern ourselves much with the reasons why he did not forward his letter to his friend, because those matters, which had been doubts before he commenced his letter, had risen to certainty before its conclusion; and he was convinced that the Pentateuch was a fable; and that it was his duty to come forward, and teach that glorious fact to those "brave minds that are yearning for light and battling for the truth!"

But there is one point in the Preface of the Bishop, on which we must bestow a short notice. We read with pain, and yet not with surprise, the way in which, in addition to his open attack on the sacred writers, the Bishop of Natal would more quietly unlearn us Christianity. To the question, "Wherewith shall I come before the Lord, and bow myself before the high God?" to which the sacrifices under the law gave some answer, the Gospel of Christ has furnished the full reply:

"Jesus saith unto him, I am the way, the truth, and the life; no man cometh unto the Father, but by Me;" "And whatsoever ye do, do all in the name of the Lord Jesus;" and "There is one God and one Mediator between God and men, the man Christ Jesus." And we need not speak of that distinguishing feature and glory of our Liturgy, that every prayer contains, or concludes with, a reference to the great High Priest of the Church, Jesus Christ the Righteous,—by whom, and whom alone, we and our prayers can find acceptance before the throne of grace.

It is, indeed, then a melancholy spectacle to see a Christian Bishop so enslaved by his infidelity that, in a solemn dedication to Almighty God of his effort to prove the Book of God a fable, he makes no more reference to the Redeemer and Mediator than Cicero or Socrates would have done, in fact, no more than if the Bishop had never heard the name of Christ.

But, indeed, from the nature of the Bishop's work, we could not expect any other course to be pursued. We should, we hope, be one of the last persons to do what we have condemned in the Bishop, "make a man an offender for a word," or deal, for a purpose, in mere conventional terms. But this is too serious a question to be passed over, without some remark on the studied way in which Bishop Colenso endeavours to banish the Lord Jesus Christ from His mediatorial throne.

We would now desire the kind indulgence of our readers on this our effort to prove the vanity of such pretensions, as those of Bishop Colenso, to impeach the wisdom and veracity of the sacred writers. And convinced that, without the blessing of God, all human exertions to do good must be in vain, and not daring to come before the living God in any other way than that of His own appointment, I would now commit this fruit of my humble labour in the cause of His truth to Him, in the name and through the mediation of Jesus Christ the righteous—man's only Mediator and Redeemer. And, if this effort to expose the folly of the show of wisdom which would deny His Revelation, prove of the least possible service to any of my fellow-men, to "GOD ONLY WISE" be all the honour and glory. Amen.

THE PRETENSIONS,

&c.

CHAPTER I.

The prophecy of Bishop Colenso respecting his Book and its influence—Predictions of other Authors respecting the reception of their Books—Doubts as to the fulfilment of the Bishop's prediction—Unhappy position in which Bishop Colenso places himself—To his Office his Book wholly indebted for any notice—The fate of Timon in reserve for Bishop Colenso.

BISHOP COLENSO predicts that his Book will be carefully read by the thinking portion of the community; who cannot but be influenced to such a degree as to compel them to join in a vigorous effort to free the Church from trammels and tyranny, and enlarge its borders, so that men of every faith and no faith, many of them openly "denying the Lord that bought them," may dwell together within its fold, "each man sitting under his vine and fig-tree, and none to make him afraid." Or, if we descend from such a beautiful description of a state of peace and happiness to the more vulgar language of our material world, each man, no matter how he may cast his vows to the idle winds, no matter how he may betray the truth which he has voluntarily sworn to maintain pure and undefiled, each such man sitting at his most comfortable table, "clothed," perhaps, "in purple and fine linen, and faring sumptuously every day" on "the loaves and fishes" of the Church to which he proves himself a traitor, and not having before his eyes the fear of the ecclesiastical tribunals; but amidst all the storms and howlings which his degenerate conduct may create, sitting "calm and unruffled as a summer sea, when not a breath of wind blows o'er its surface," in the full enjoyment of all the good things of time and sense, obtained too by the money received from the Church, which, Judas-like, he has betrayed, and betrayed with a kiss.

Would not this be a delightful state of things, if only we could look forward with certainty to the fulfilment of the prediction of Bishop Colenso as to the effect which his volume is to produce in the country? Indeed, he predicts this result of his work as the only hope of the continuance of the Church. And this Right Reverend proprietor of all wisdom and truth is not willing to grant the said Church a lease of even five years, if his scandalous production do not produce the very wonderful effect which he so confidently predicts.

Well! Bishop Colenso is not the first man who, on sending a book into the world, sent it forth with a prophecy respecting the reception which it would obtain. But some men, and very great men, were, we must say, much more modest than our Right Reverend Author—men, too, whose writings have come down to us unimpaired by "the wasting hand of time."

Julius Cæsar, as Lord Bacon remarks, with a modesty well befitting true greatness, on sending forth his book, called that bare commentaries, which turned out to be one of the noblest histories in the world.

Horace knew the value of his writings, but, nevertheless, he speaks of his book as if destined merely to be thumbed by school-boys, and even to be carried into the back streets where pepper and all kinds of spices, and whatever was wont to be wrapped up in useless paper, were sold.

Notwithstanding, however, this modesty, he does, we admit, exclaim,—

> "Non omnis moriar, multaque pars mei
> Vitabit Libitinam."

And he also wrote his

> "Exegi monumentum æro perennius."

But, for all this, Horace did not make the existence of the wisdom and philosophy of time to depend on the reception which his volume was to receive. And we do think, without any disrespect to Bishop Colenso, that Horace will be read when the unhappy volume of the Bishop will be clean forgotten, like a dead man out of mind.

Now we venture to predict that the result will be very different from Bishop Colenso's opinion and prophecy of his book and its effect on society. We believe, nay, are as confident as if we had power not only to survey the past, but to dive into the future, that five years will elapse, and many times five years after that the tongue and hand of Bishop Colenso shall be silent and powerless in the grave, and all things will go on as now in their regular course: the Church will be in existence—though in the midst of corruption and jobbing of preferments—even as the bush though surrounded by the devouring and yet harmless flame. Of her children, some will hear her voice only to prove "the terrible waste of moral agents by themselves;" while on the other hand, many will receive, day by day, Sabbath by Sabbath, and year by year, in her ordinances and means of grace, the bread of life and the water of salvation, to support them in their journey through this barren wilderness of time, until they reach in safety and health that land of promise, where they shall hunger and thirst no more.

We cannot place any faith in the prophecy of the Bishop. But, rather, reasoning from the past, and looking to the good hand of Providence as its defence and guide, we believe that, as the Church of England has survived the fiery trials of persecution from the earliest times, under Pagans, Romans, Saxons, Papists, and Puritans, so it will survive the Book and prophecy of Bishop Colenso; and so survive, as to hold forth the lamp of truth, and hold fast the form of sound words, and present a barrier against the efforts of all those who, whether bishops, clergy, or laity, would introduce into its fold the teaching of heresy, schism, or infidelity of any kind, or in any degree.

But although we thus believe and conclude, yet it is indeed a sad spectacle to see a servant of the Church send forth from such a commanding position as the Episcopal throne, a book in the least degree calculated to overthrow the faith of any of the family of God, "of souls which were the purchase and price of Christ's blood [1]," and yet retain the position and emoluments of that Church which his volume has the tendency, but, like the spear of Priam—a "telum imbelle et sine ictu"—not the power to undermine and destroy.

We do not desire to write in any disrespectful manner of Bishop Colenso, although we should feel for him some respect if he had laid aside his sacred

---

[1] Jeremy Taylor.

robes, and had surrendered the emoluments of his high office. But we cannot give flattering titles, and therefore we must say, that to his position in the Church, and to it alone, must this book of Bishop Colenso be indebted for any notice that it may command. Were it not for this position, a work of such ludicrous self-sufficiency in identifying his notions with philosophy and truth, a work which exhibits such absence of any thing original in its objections, and which deals in such petty cavils, which shows the littleness of seeking to discover spots on the face of the Sun of Revelation, instead of admiring the blaze of light and glory which that sun has shed upon a dark and benighted world,—such a book, divested of the accidents of the high and holy position of the writer, would soon share the fate of which Timon complains so bitterly in his noisy and scolding address to Jupiter.

Having rated Jupiter well for allowing bad men to have the upper hand, Timon instances his own case, that he raised many of the Athenians from poverty to great prosperity; assisted all who were in need; and poured out his wealth in heaps for the benefit of his friends. "But now, since by such means I have become poor, I am not any longer known by them, nor do they take the least notice of me; fellows, who not only lately trembled in my presence, but adored me, and hung upon my nod. And if I chance to meet any of them by the way, they pass me by as they would the fallen-down tombstone of some one long dead, which has been worn out by time, and without even stopping to read the inscription."

Like Timon, Bishop Colenso owes to his station the notice which his Book receives; and so long as he retains his high position he will command friends and flatterers; but as the great Philosopher reminds us, many men are "much more abundantly mortal in their pursuits than in their bodies." So Bishop Colenso will prove to his bitter mortification: when stripped of the robes which he has degraded by his infidelity, and shorn of his position and its emoluments, he will experience the fate of Timon; and his friends and flatterers will pass him also by as they would the fallen-down gravestone of the neglected dead, as unmindful of himself and his infidel production as if he or it never had any existence. And the worst of this bitter trial will be, that the Church of England, whose fall was so confidently predicted by the Bishop and his followers, unless the Bishop's philosophy were to be received as the creed of the Church, will be found still alive.

CHAPTER II.

The Bishop's mode of arguing from words and figures to neglect of the substance so signified—His method contrary to all principles of sound reasoning—Vanity of such assumption of wisdom as exhibited by the Bishop—Apology made for the conduct of the Bishop—Flippancy of self-styled Philosophers—Improper appointments of such men to the Offices of Public Instructors.

In his noble work, "The Wisdom of God in Creation," the learned Mr. Ray quotes "a wise and observant Prelate" who remarks, "That learning which consists only in the form and pedagogy of arts, or the critical notions upon words and phrases, hath in it this intrinsical imperfection, that it is only so far to be esteemed as it conduceth to the knowledge of things, being in itself but a kind of pedantry, apt to infect a man with such odd humours of pride and affectation and curiosity, as will render him unfit for any great employment. Words being but the images of matter, to be wholly given up to the study of these, what is it but Pygmalion's frenzy, to fall in love with a picture or image?"

Bishop Colenso, we are sorry to say, does indeed labour under this Pygmalion disease; for, instead of dealing with the substance or truth designed, he is wholly occupied with mere signs by which that substance or truth is represented to the mind.

The Bishop seizes upon certain forms of speech and figures and statistics,—of which last we never hear without thinking of the remark attributed to Mr. Canning, that he had the greatest horror of men who dealt in statistics,—and to all these the Bishop objects; and, because those forms of speech or figures or statistics are not as he would have written or ordered, or else do not square with his ideas, concludes that therefore the work in which they are contained is pure fable, and the other writings, which bear the same name, are no better.

Than such a mode of arguing, for we cannot dignify it with the name of reasoning, there cannot be any thing more offensive to all the rules of logic, and therefore to common sense, on the ground of its self-conceit as well as utter emptiness. Besides, a man should show some modesty when he comes into opposition with and sits in judgment on the belief and testimony of the learned, wise, and good of all ages and nations. "I do not see this in the light in which others have done and continue to do, therefore it is all pure invention, no better than 'the baseless fabric of a vision.' I say this; and though all mankind should assert the contrary, yet what I say must stand—for it and it only is Philosophy and Truth."

This kind of vanity and assumption may, as it often does, awe weak minds into subjection, but it is poor trifling with reason. It reminds us of the excuse given by the madman to a friend, who on finding him in a Lunatic Asylum asked, "What brought you here?" "Well, you know that I always maintained that all men were mad, and all men maintained that I was mad, and they had the majority, and here I am."

If Bishop Colenso felt himself called to the special mission of groping for difficulties in the mere detail, and, if we may so speak, trifling parts of such a grand and surpassingly glorious whole or scheme of Revelation, before proceeding to such an extremity as to denounce the writing a fable and the writer a fool or deceiver, he might have confessed his inability to solve such difficulties. If he had bethought himself, that in order to fully understand all mere accidentals in which that Revelation may be clothed, or even the difficulties which it in common with the Book of Nature must be expected to contain, he should have lived in the days of the Compilers of those Sacred Writings, and have been familiar with all their customs, manners, and varied use of words, then he would have rendered proper homage to reason and have done honour to himself. But when from *his* difficulties as to one point, *his* unbelief as to another, and from *his* ignorance of both sides, or of the whole of the question, he concludes that the Pentateuch is a fable, then he does violence to all principles of sound reasoning, and places himself in as senseless and ludicrous a light as did the poor man who worked himself into the madhouse by his unceasing efforts to convince mankind that he himself was the only sane man.

And when, moreover, Bishop Colenso deals with not the common records of time, but with records, which, to obtain his position and its advantages, he has solemnly pledged his faith and honour to be the Records of Heaven, the writings of men "who spake as they were moved by the Holy Ghost"—then we are further of opinion that it would have been much more becoming in him to have paid attention to the words, "Put off thy shoes from off thy feet, for the place whereon thou standest is holy ground." If Doctor Colenso were other than a man occupying the place of a Christian Bishop,—if he were a layman or an avowed infidel,—we should not use such language, which would be out of place, as would be even the least notice of his foolish production.

We heard this apology made for the strange conduct of Bishop Colenso, that the Bishop never studied the learning connected with his profession; but that his mind was wholly given to mathematics and figures, and that he split on the rock of expecting to find demonstrative evidence in every particular.

We give this apology as we heard it made; but we cannot admit it to have any weight. There are, it is too true, men who study mathematics as if that science were itself the end instead of being the mere means to an end; and who so regard the subject as if the whole business of life, and all the philosophy of time, consisted in "doing a problem:" thus making a noble science no better than a Chinese puzzle. And experience proves that such men, as they are always the most self-sufficient, so they are universally the most useless members of society. They are so wrapped up in their exalted opinion of themselves, and in the blind and absurd notion, that their views and opinions, and philosophy and truth are all one and the same, that it is not possible to convince them of the truth or value of any thing that does not square with their own contracted ideas.

In the days of our youth, and at such an age when a shallow speech from a "philosopher" might have sown in our breast the seeds of infidelity, we heard of a lecture at one of our Universities, and by a Reverend

Professor. Two private gentlemen, friends of the writer of these remarks, were present; who on their return from their visit to the seat of learning, related the following dialogue, as having taken place after the lecture. The lecture, we may state, made some reference to a subject on which the madness of the philosophers of that day turned,—for those philosophers, like other members of society, are mad,—and as the symptom of madness in the people varies, showing itself one day in hunting down this hobby, and another day some other, so at the time in question the madness of the philosophers showed its symptoms in proving a wonderful fact—the discovery of a pre-Adamite woman. This their advance in some of the Sciences, of Geology in particular, caused them to know as a fact, which of course made the account of Creation given by Moses a fable, and Moses himself an ignorant fool and deceiver.

But to our narrative,—"Thank you, Mr. Professor, for your excellent lecture; but, by-the-bye, did not that part," naming a certain portion, " contradict Moses?" " Oh," replied the Reverend Professor, " if Moses contradict science——" And in imitation, we suppose, of Virgil's famous " Quos Ego" in Neptune's scolding attack on Æolus, he broke off the sentence with a snap of his fingers. Or, it may be, that the Reverend Professor followed the rule of the true sublime, as laid down by Longinus: to state so much as to give the idea, and leave much to be conceived; which then, if literally translated, would stand thus: " If Moses contradict," we will not say science, for Moses knew more of science than did or do any of such empty fools; but " If Moses contradict my views and opinions, why then he must go to the winds."

And yet such, by the just verdict of St. Paul, are the fools — " professing themselves to be wise they became fools"—who are in too many instances put into the places of guides and instructors of the nation. And such the men, who, in the opinion of the unthinking and shallow of every rank and degree, are too often accounted the more eminent philosophers in proportion to their vanity, their smattering of science, and empty though high-sounding pretensions. But the homely proverb speaks truth,—"The empty barrel sounds loudest."

CHAPTER III.

The case of the Zulu—The immediate cause of the Bishop's Book—The Bishop's zeal for truth at the expense of the Redeemer and Sacred Writers—No honour to the Father apart from honour to the Son of God—Unsoundness of reasoning from objections against positive evidence—Way in which such arguing treated by the Redeemer—The Bishop's fact—The method adopted by such men of proving things by things themselves unproved—Test of the Bishop's mode of concluding—In what its fallacy consists—Example of Jeremiah.

BEFORE we examine the several points of detail, the difficulties which prove to the mind of Bishop Colenso that the Pentateuch is a fable, we must consider the case stated by him as the immediate cause of his coming forward as the great Champion of "The Truth;" that is, his own notions. Besides, this case is the only part of the Book of Bishop Colenso, which deals in any principle of reasoning; the other parts being the mere and minute detail of the mode of arguing which this case propounds.

This case imposed on the Bishop the duty of enlightening a dark and ignorant world, which dreamt for ages that it knew the truth,—but which was under a very grievous mistake; a mistake, however, to be excused, as it had not examined these subjects with any degree of attention or criticism, or with the advance in the knowledge of some of the sciences, which the Bishop states that he made since his departure from England. As therefore all the great, learned, and good men, who have lived in time past, and whose writings and memory we have been accustomed to regard with reverence, had not such advantages, and were not so accustomed to bring every thing to the high standard of plus and minus, and lines and angles,—and had not, we presume, the capacity to take in science, more especially that of Geology, in the same or any thing like the same degree as our Modern Critics and Philosophers of the School of which Bishop Colenso is now the Principal,—why then their ignorance and mistake may be accounted for and pardoned!

This case to which the country stands so indebted for his Work is thus stated by Bishop Colenso:— "While translating the story of the Flood, I have had a simple-minded but intelligent native,—one with the docility of a child, but the reasoning powers of mature age,—look up and ask, 'Is all that true? Do you really believe that all this happened thus; that all the beasts, and birds, and creeping things upon the earth, large and small, from hot countries and cold, came thus by pairs and entered into the Ark with Noah? And did Noah gather food for them *all*, for the beasts and birds of prey as well as for the rest?'"

"My heart," the Bishop writes, "answered in the words of the Prophet: 'Shall a man speak lies in the name of the Lord?' Zech. xiii. 3. I dared not do so. My own knowledge of some branches of science, of Geology in particular, had been much increased since I left England; and I now know for certain, on geological grounds, a fact, of which I had only misgivings before, viz.—that a *Universal Deluge*, such as the Bible manifestly speaks of, could not possibly have taken place in the way described in the Book of Genesis, not to mention other difficulties which the story contains."

And so the Bishop, knowing all this history of the deluge to be a fable, though the Redeemer Himself, and St. Peter, St. Paul, and others of the sacred writers, dealt with and quoted the history recorded by Moses as truth,—yet Bishop Colenso, knowing far better than even those authorities, continues, "I felt that I dared not, as a servant of the God of Truth, urge my brother to believe that which I did not myself believe, which I knew to be untrue, as a matter-of-fact, historical narrative."

We wonder that, when the Bishop wrote thus, it did not occur to his mind, that in making the Son of God "a liar,"—for Christ bears unqualified testimony to the deluge as recorded by Moses,—he was only mocking his Maker by professing to do such honour to the God of Truth, and also by his own confession to seek to make infidels of the sons of men. For in our old-fashioned Christianity we have always read and believed the words,—"He that honoureth not the Son, honoureth not the Father which hath sent Him." But to return to the question.

We must confess that we should have looked for a better system of reasoning, in a man who claims to be a master of science, than to reason or rather cavil from objections and difficulties against a fact; for in spite of the Bishop's advance in some of the sciences, and his consequent certain knowledge of *his* fact, which proves beyond doubt the whole account by Moses to be a mere fable, yet we may, we humbly think, conclude that the truth of the history recorded by Moses does, and will stand against the lately learned fact of Bishop Colenso. Under these circumstances we say, then, that this arguing, not reasoning, from difficulties and objections against any statement sustained by an overwhelming weight of positive evidence, is not only contrary to all idea of sound reasoning, which reverses the Bishop's mode, and makes objections give place to positive evidence; but, we repeat, such mode of arguing is not what we should have expected from a man who has the reputation of being a mathematician.

Such mode of treating a question is the same as that adopted by Nicodemus, when our Lord laid down the important truth, "Except a man be born again, he cannot enter the kingdom of God." "How can these things be? Can a man enter a second time into his mother's womb and be born?" But the only reply of Christ was to repeat the truth, as was His custom, without turning aside to discuss the objections and difficulties which blinded the eyes of Nicodemus; though, on another remarkable occasion, He did explain difficulties to His disciples, which He would not notice when used as cavils by the unbelieving Jews.

We hope that the Bishop will pardon us if, while on the subject of *his* fact, which proves the writing by Moses to be a fable, we give our view as to the category in which his fact may be placed. We do not then hesitate to place it in the category of Junius, who, in one of his letters to Sir William Draper, writes, "In the first place, Sir William, your facts are false." Or, to come down from the sublime to the ridiculous, in the category of the Popish priest who, some thirty years ago, broke out and disturbed a public meeting by repeatedly calling out, "That's a false fact!"

Now, to any one who is not moved by the vain

pretensions of such philosophers, but who searches into questions, it will be evident that the facts of most of such men are built only on their own ignorance and assumption. Did any of those men who, like Bishop Colenso, would prove Moses a fool and deceiver, ever yet establish their facts any other way than by things themselves unproved?—which mode at last resolves all into this: "Such is my assertion, and therefore it is truth;" arguing in the vicious circle, which Stillingfleet, in his exposure of the reasoning in behalf of Papal infallibility, describes as John giving a character to Thomas, and Thomas in return giving a character to John.

Thus Bishop Colenso proves *his* fact to be a fact, because he made, since his departure from England, such advance in some of the sciences as taught him this for certain. And then his fact in return proves that Moses was a fool or worse, and the writing which bears his name a fable. And thus all is to be resolved into this: that such is the fact, because Bishop Colenso asserts that it is the fact.

And now what need was there of all the trouble which the Bishop took in writing a book, which has caused no little excitement, and which has exposed him to such just ridicule, as we believe is on every side bestowed on his poor production? The whole question could have been settled in a few words, or if the Bishop desired to rush into print on the subject, by a single advertisement in the "Times" to this effect:—

"I, John William Colenso, D.D., Bishop of Natal, hereby give notice, to all whom it may concern, that the writings of Moses are a fable, and Moses a fool and deceiver! And this is the truth, because I know a fact, and therefore declare that it is the truth.

"(Signed) J. W. NATAL."

Surely this would have been the shortest and easiest way to have settled the question.

But let us now, as Launcelot Gobbo says, "try conclusions" with Bishop Colenso, and look into his mode of establishing facts by arguing from objections or difficulties against what is sustained by positive evidence. Suppose that we were to visit the diocese of Natal, not to teach revealed religion or to sow the seeds of infidelity, but solely to instruct the people in the Book of Nature. And let us further suppose that, in discoursing on the sun, moon, and stars, we were to inform some native of their magnitude, their distances, and inhabitants, that all those bodies were a collection of worlds, like our earth, hanging upon nothing; and that this man—for instance the Bishop's inquirer—were to look up at us and ask, "Do you believe all this? Do you believe that this earth hangs upon nothing, or that any such thing could take place? This is contrary to a fact which I know, and plain common sense proves all this to be a fable." Now, would this mode of arguing be unreasonable on the part of a poor untutored Zulu? Certainly not. But would this mode of objecting prove the Book of Nature to be a fable? And yet such is precisely the mode of *reasoning* by which the Bishop of Natal endeavours to overthrow the faith of men, and establish infidelity by proclaiming the writings of Moses a fable, and Moses himself a deceiver, for to this point we must always necessarily come.

The fallacy of this wretched system of so-called reasoning, lies in the vanity of measuring the infinitely wise and Almighty Creator and Ruler of the Universe by our standard of folly and feebleness, concluding that, because we cannot see how or why such or such a thing could be done, and because we could not ourselves do such, therefore it could not be done, no, not even by the All-wise and Omnipotent Himself.

We must, we suppose, take heed how we presume to instruct a Bishop; and therefore we shall not stop to point out the way in which, if a believer in what he professed to obtain his position, the Bishop should, and in perfect harmony with philosophy could, have replied to the not unreasonable question of the poor Zulu—not unreasonable in a man who had to learn that the Bible is the Revelation of the living and true God. But we cannot deny ourselves a reference to the Prophet Jeremiah, to show the way in which he sought to solve, not merely objections, but, so far as man could see or act, impossibilities which surrounded the path of duty.

Jerusalem was in the hands of the enemy. The inhabitants were captives in a land not their own. At such a crisis Jeremiah received the command to buy a certain field, to invest not merely his belief in the word of his Maker, but to invest that which has been the *fons et origo*, the *irritamenta malorum* of the human race, to invest his money in the purchase of land in a city and country in a state of hopeless ruin under the wasting domination of the most powerful earthly monarch. Jeremiah felt the difficulty in all its force, but he bought the field; and then, in a most beautiful prayer and pious remonstrance, he thus stays himself on the word of his Maker:

"Ah Lord God! behold, Thou hast made the heaven and the earth by Thy great power and stretched out arm, and there is nothing too hard for Thee: Thou showest loving-kindness unto thousands, and recompensest the iniquity of the fathers into the bosom of their children after them: the Great, the Mighty God, the LORD of hosts, is His name, great in counsel, and mighty in work: for Thine eyes are open upon all the ways of the sons of men: to give every one according to his ways, and according to the fruit of his doings: which hast set signs and wonders in the land of Egypt, even unto this day, and in Israel, and among other men; and hast made Thee a name, as at this day; and hast brought forth Thy people Israel out of the land of Egypt with signs, and with wonders, and with a strong hand, and with a stretched out arm, and with great terror; and hast given them this land, which Thou didst swear unto their fathers to give them, a land flowing with milk and honey; and they came in, and possessed it; but they obeyed not Thy voice, neither walked in Thy law; they have done nothing of all that Thou commandedst them to do: therefore Thou hast caused all this evil to come upon them: behold the mounts, they are come into the city to take it; and the city is given into the hand of the Chaldeans, that fight against it, because of the sword, and of the famine, and of the pestilence: and what Thou hast spoken is come to pass; and, behold, Thou seest it. And Thou hast said unto me, O LORD GOD, Buy thee the field for money, and take witnesses; for (or though) the city is given into the hands of the Chaldeans."

"Then," the Prophet continues, "came the word of the LORD unto Jeremiah, saying, Behold, I am the LORD, the GOD of all flesh: Is there any thing too hard for Me?" This answer was enough. Jeremiah flung to the winds all his difficulties and objections. He believed the word of his God, though he could not see the end. Having subscribed the purchase-roll, and bought the field, he patiently awaited the promised result. This was conduct worthy of the man, and dignifying to the mind, showing it in its true light: never so great, as when bowing down to and acting on the word of the Infinitely Wise.

But it may be that, in the judgment of Bishop Colenso, Jeremiah was a weak man who took things on trust, and who certainly had not made any critical examination of the sacred writings; for, had he done so, he never could have adopted in such a pointed manner the Mosiac account of the Exodus, and especially of creation, as he does in ascribing to GOD the creation of His own Universe, notwithstanding the many difficulties which, by the Bishop's logic, would have proved such creation a mere fable; and notwithstanding the fact, that some very clever men, called philosophers, had maintained the very opposite, and had most clearly proved the fact—one of the Bishop's facts—to the satisfaction of themselves and followers, that the Universe was created and governed by chance.

Well, be it so. But, without discussing this question, we had rather cast in our lot with Jeremiah in the dungeon than live in the palace of any Bishop on earth, and have to answer for the want of candour and truth, the vanity and self-sufficiency, and the fearful sin of publishing a wretched work, calculated at least, and that by the confession and desire of its author, to make an infidel of even a solitary individual of the race of Adam.

CHAPTER IV.

Difficulties in the Scriptures—The Nativity—The Death of Christ—The Resurrection—Bishop Colenso proves too much—Resurrection of the body contrary to our experience, though preached by Nature—Not known to the Heathen world—Reception of St. Paul at Athens for preaching the Resurrection—On Bishop Colenso's principle the difficulty of this article of faith would prove the whole Bible a fable—The confession of Aristotle as to the insufficiency of the light of Nature, commended as a lesson to Bishop Colenso's School of Philosophers.

SHOULD Bishop Colenso ever arrive at the end of his proposed work of showing to the human race the folly of past ages, and how much of the Revelation of God his advance in some of the sciences will allow him to authorize mankind henceforth to believe, we may imagine other difficulties and objections to arise during his critical examination and reform of the Holy Scriptures.

And should the Bishop ever return to his diocese of Natal, which for the sake of the benighted people who were unhappily confided to his care, and also for the sake of common decency, we trust he never will be permitted to do, we might in such case picture to our minds the following scene :—The Bishop translating the history of the Nativity, assisted by his simple-minded but intelligent Zulu, and the Zulu looking up at the Bishop and asking, "Do you believe all this? Do you really think that all this is true?" On his principle of arguing the Bishop could not have replied to such a question, but must have joined the Zulu in concluding the whole account to be a fable and a lie—a lie, too, spoken in the name of the Lord.

Again : suppose the Bishop instructing his Zulu in

the doctrine of the death of Christ; not the death of a man, with which all are so painfully familiar, but the death of Christ as the Lord of life and glory; and the death of Christ, not to set us an example how to die, but the death for or instead of us. Now, might not the Zulu reply in a similar manner to the answer of the Eastern idolater, whose religion was to prostrate himself in adoration before the glorious orb of day? When told that he was to believe in Christ, because He died for us, "Died! then I had rather believe in the sun that never dies than in a God that was mortal."

We defy Bishop Colenso to give on his principles of arguing any other answer in this case also than that the whole account is fable and falsehood. It may be very well, that insufficiency of even repentance to atone for sin, and the necessity and value of mediation, are taught by the daily experience of life. But the great philosophers of old never saw this, though thus every hour before their eyes, or they would not have accounted the preaching of Christ crucified as the merest foolishness.

Or, take the case of the Resurrection of the Lord Jesus. "Do you believe all this? How can this be true? Do you really believe that any thing so contrary to our experience could happen, that a man once dead should ever rise again?"

Now, here too, according to the mode of arguing adopted by Bishop Colenso, there could not be any reply to these questions of the Zulu. All these objections are founded on their opposition to, and contradiction of, the common experience of mankind; and *reasoning* in this way, taught by one who made such advance in some of the sciences since his departure from England, we must conclude that the whole history of the Resurrection of the Lord Jesus is mere fable, and that the Evangelists wrote "lies in the name of the Lord."

It is also in this case very true that, if men were not by nature so wholly blind as to spiritual things, they could learn that death is the way to life, or, in other words, that resurrection, though contrary to our experience, is not so contrary to the course of all things. Nature, though a silent yet most eloquent orator, preaches in several ways the doctrine of resurrection. And it is equally true, that if we closely examine the nature of resurrection, it cannot present any difficulties, save only in reference to the agent or to the subject of action; difficulties, which in a question that presupposes the interference of Omnipotence, such being the only ground for the belief of the doctrine, cannot for a moment be allowed. Bishop Pearson thus states both these points in his masterly and vigorous style:

"The day dies into night, and is buried in silence and in darkness; in the next morning it appeareth again and reviveth, opening the grave of darkness, rising from the dead of night: this is the diurnal resurrection. As the day dies into night, so doth the summer into winter: the sap is said to descend into the root, and there it lies buried in the ground; the earth is covered with snow, or crusted with frost, and becomes a general sepulchre: when the spring appeareth, all begin to rise; the plants and flowers peep out of their graves, revive, and grow, and flourish: this is the annual resurrection. The corn by which we live, and for want of which we perish with famine, is notwithstanding cast upon the earth and buried in the ground with a design that it may corrupt, and being corrupted may revive and multiply; our bodies are fed with this constant experiment, and we continue this present life by a succession of resurrections. Thus all things are repaired by corrupting, are preserved by perishing, and revive by dying. And can we think that man, the Lord of all these things, which thus die and revive for him, should be detained in death as never to live again? Is it imaginable that God should thus restore all things to man, and not restore man to Himself?"

And as to the possibility he writes:—

"Now when we say the resurrection is possible, we say not it is so to men or angels, or any creature of a limited knowledge or finite power, but we attribute it to God, 'with whom nothing is impossible:' His understanding is infinite; He knoweth all the men which ever lived since the foundation, or shall live unto the dissolution of the world; He knoweth whereof all things are made, from what 'dust' we came, into what dust we shall return. . . . . He which numbereth the sands of the sea, knoweth all the scattered bones, seeth into all the graves and tombs, searcheth all the repositories and dormitories in the earth, knoweth what dust belongeth to each body, what body to each soul.

"Again: as His all-seeing eye observeth every particle of dissolved and corrupted man, so doth He also see and know all ways and means by which these scattered parts should be united, by which this ruined fabric should be recomposed; He knoweth how every bone should be brought to its old neighbour bone, how every sinew may be re-embroidered on it; He understandeth what are the proper parts to be conjoined, what is the proper gluten by which they may become united. The resurrection, therefore, cannot be impossible in relation to the agent upon any deficiency of knowledge how to effect it.

"And as the wisdom of God is infinite, so the power of this agent is illimited: for God is as much omnipotent as omniscient. There can be no opposition made against Him, because all power is His; nor can He receive a check against whom there is no resistance: all creatures must not only suffer, but do what He will have them; they are not only passively, but actively, obediential. There is no atom of the dust or ashes but must be where it pleaseth God, and be applied and make up what and how it seemeth good to Him. The resurrection, therefore, cannot be impossible in relation unto God upon any disability to effect it; and, consequently, there is no impossibility in reference to the agent, or Him who is to raise us.

"Secondly, the resurrection is not impossible *in relation to the patient,* because where we look upon the power of God, nothing can be impossible but that which involveth a contradiction; and there can be no contradiction in this, that he which was, and now is not, should hereafter be what before he was. It is so far from a repugnancy, that it rather containeth a rational and apparent possibility, that man who was once dust, becoming dust, should become man again. Whatsoever we lose in death is not lost to God; as no creature could be made out of nothing but by Him, so can it not be reduced into nothing but by the same: though, therefore, the parts of the body of man be dissolved, yet they perish not; they lose not their own entity when they part with their relation to humanity: they are laid up in the secret places, and lodged in the chambers of nature; and it is no more a contradiction that they should become the parts of the same body of man to which they did belong, than that after his death they should become the parts of any other body, as we see they do. Howsoever they are scattered, and howsoever lodged, they are within the knowledge and power of God. . . . . When there was no man, God made him of the earth; and, therefore, when he returns to the earth, the same God can make him man again."

We therefore conclude, that as Christ rose from the dead, so He became the first-fruits of them that slept, or who shall sleep in the grave; and that though when we die we seem lost to being, we are not lost to God; but, as Pearson writes, our dust is laid up in the vast dormitories of nature, in the chambers of the grave, there to await the summons of Him who at first formed us out of dust to awake from our sleep, and stand before His great white throne of judgment.

But although all this be truth thus most clearly taught in the Book of Nature, yet resurrection of the body is wholly contrary to our experience; and that it is so contrary to our experience, and that it never entered into the minds of the heathen philosophers, as indeed it never would have entered into our minds, but for the Gospel of Him who has brought life and immortality to light, may be proved not only by the voice of history, but by the reception which the preaching of St. Paul experienced at the hands of the philosophers of Athens. They heard him so long as he preached of rewards and punishments in a future state, for all that doctrine they knew in common with the Jew or the Christian, and which may be known without any other revelation than the light of nature.

It was only when Paul preached unto them " one Jesus and the Resurrection," that they mocked and denounced him as a babbler. " What will this babbler say?" "He seemeth to be a setter forth of strange gods." "This babbler!" said the philosophers of the great Apostle of the Gentiles; this fool and deceiver of mankind! as Bishop Colenso *proves* Moses who was one of the wisest and greatest of men.

Where are those philosophers now? What were their names? Where are their writings? And as to "this babbler," what is his name? What his never-dying immortal labours for the good of the human race? And what his splendid writings? which have been the rich feast of countless millions of intelligent minds, as they shall be of millions of intelligent minds yet unborn, even until time itself shall be no more. And yet this wonderful man was a believer in the fable of Moses! Bishop Colenso may here, in the philosophers of Athens who denounced "this babbler," read the fate of himself and his disgraceful thrusting of his loathsome infidelity on the public mind.

But to return to the question. Where, moreover, shall we look? Shall we cast up our eyes unto the heavens, or look upon the earth beneath, and not find difficulty upon difficulty? Into the wisdom of this state of trial it is not our business now to enter; suffice it to say, that all is mystery and difficulty; not merely apart from, but even when viewed in the light of that Revelation which a merciful Creator has given to the sons of men. Here "we know in part," but only "in part," even at our best estate; "now we see through a glass darkly," only darkly. And as to the scheme of Redemption, it is a mystery which, the Apostle writes, the very "angels desire to look into." And we ourselves are perhaps the greatest wonder and mystery, and the prime difficulty in creation. Must we then from such mystery and difficulty, and from our utter ignorance of the reason and wisdom of such a state of things, conclude that all this state of things, even our own existence, is mere fable?

And yet such is the very way in which Bishop Colenso would overthrow the truth of the "Holy Scriptures," and leave the human race without that Revelation for which the good and great of the heathen world sighed; and cast us as forlorn wanderers on the earth without one ray of light or hope to guide and cheer us on our journey through this dark and dreary wilderness of time; dark and dreary indeed, without that lamp of truth, which Bishop Colenso endeavours to extinguish.

Aristotle was a great man ; and it would be a happy thing for themselves, if our self-styled philosophers of Christian times, who usurp all wisdom to themselves, would learn a lesson of humility from the reported dying confession of that great man who governed the world for centuries by his philosophy :—" Polluted I entered into this world ; in anxiety I have lived ; full of confusion I take my departure : Cause of causes, have mercy upon me !"

When we read such a mournful testimony from such a great mind, how forcibly we are reminded of the words,—" But blessed are your eyes, for they see ; and your ears, for they hear. For verily I say unto you, That many prophets and righteous men have desired to see those things which ye see, and have not seen them ; and to hear those things which ye hear, and have not heard them."

But now, leaving further examination of this mode of arguing from difficulties and objections by which the Bishop of Natal proves the writings of Moses, and consequently the Bible, a fable,—we say consequently, not only because the same mode would overturn any revelation, but because the other parts of the Sacred Volume must stand or fall with this fable,—let us turn to another view of this subject, and of the modesty and philosophy of Bishop Colenso.

CHAPTER V.

The Bishop's reply to the question of the Zulu—No difficulty in the question when rightly considered—Endowment of irrational creatures with instinct as great a difficulty to us, but no difficulty to the Creator—The Question of the Almighty on this point—No difficulty to justify the conclusion of Bishop Colenso—Other methods of solving his difficulty than the Bishop's charge of falsehood against Moses—Moses did not invent the history of the Deluge, Creation, or of Religion—Longinus's Remark on Moses' account of Creation—Heathen accounts of the Deluge—Ovid—Lucian—The only question—Whether Moses or Bishop Colenso be "the more credible."

BISHOP COLENSO states, that, when the poor Zulu asked him, "Is all that true? Do you really believe that all this happened thus?" &c., the Bishop asked himself, "Shall a man speak lies in the name of the Lord?" and he adds, "I dared not do so." And as he knew a fact which proved the statement of Moses to be a fable, he resolved to so instruct the human race. It is not our object to do more than our title sets forth, consider the pretensions of Bishop Colenso to impeach the wisdom and veracity of the inspired writer. But had we been at the ear of the Bishop, we could have asked him a few questions, which, if they did not make those things cease to be difficulties, would at least have shown that the difficulties in question did not furnish ground for denouncing the narrative as pure falsehood.

As to difficulty, there is none, can be none whatever, so far as the mere fact recorded. Any difficulty exists only in our minds, because to our minds such things do naturally present difficulties; for they are contrary to our common experience. But when we view those questions apart from our finite minds, and our contracted experience, there is not any more difficulty than, to repeat the illustration already given, to stretch out the north over the empty space, and to hang the earth upon nothing.

Nor is there any miracle, or need of miracle, so far as the account of the animals and birds seeking refuge in the Ark. It was a most remarkable providential arrangement; but, after all, not any suspension of the order of nature, such being that in which a miracle consists; and certainly no ground of difficulty to the Supreme Being, any more, as we say, than hanging the earth upon nothing, or than the endowment of animals and birds with that unerring and astonishing instinct which they exhibit. Now that instinct none but the Maker of all things could bestow; and so we find the existence of that instinct referred to by the Creator to show His power, and to bring down the inflated pride of man: " Doth the hawk fly by thy wisdom, and stretch her wings toward the south?"

The latter part of which question shows, on a small scale, what took place in the Ark, and what takes place every year; viz. the exercise of the instinct bestowed by the Creator, which causes animals and birds to forsake certain places on impending changes, and move to other parts of the earth for the preservation of their lives.

Far be it from our mind to write as if we were obliged to apologize for, or explain the acts of the Creator. We examine the only question here,—" Is the Bible a revelation from God to man?" And if it be, we acknowledge its truth and bow before its statements all the time that we may in that very revelation find scope, and it is a vast ocean, for the most active exercise and enlarged operations of the mind. But we state these matters by the way, to show that even what took place in the Ark is only what is being continually carried on in the Divine government of the world: that there was not, could not be any difficulty in the fact recorded, or difficulty in the thing itself, any more than in the creation and endowment of the creatures with existence or instinct; and certainly not any difficulty on which to found the most illogical conclusions of Bishop Colenso.

But it does seem very strange that Bishop Colenso should not have exercised some reflection, and have shown before the public some respect for the character of Moses; but that quite forgetting every consideration, except the love of singularity and praise of men, while proclaiming his own abhorrence of a lie, he should have left the world to draw the conclusion, on his testimony confirmed by his fact, that Moses was guilty of that base conduct from which, he informs us, his own mind revolted; and that Moses did write an untruth, was, in fact, guilty of a lie, and,—worse than all,—a lie spoken in the name of the Lord.

We very humbly suggest, that there were other courses open to our Christian Bishop to escape from *his* difficulty, without leaving the charge of wilful and impious falsehood at the door of such a great and honoured servant of God.

Now Moses did not invent the history of Creation, or of the Deluge in particular, or of religion. He only wrote the history of those subjects. All these were matters of fact, which he, in common with others, has recorded. And we need scarcely remark that religion, natural or revealed,—we do not speak of views or doctrines, but of religion itself,—does not owe its existence in the world to the writings of any man; all writers have dealt with it as in existence, as a mere fact. So much, then, as to the Mosaic history of one or all of those questions.

As to the account given by Moses of Creation, and to which the other sacred writings so constantly refer, we may mention as an interesting point for the mere English reader, that the author of the grand work on "the Sublime,"—of whom it has been said,

> "So true to Nature's laws,
> And is himself the great sublime he draws,"—

Longinus, selects the account of Creation by Moses as a striking instance of the true sublime. The heathen writers in their accounts laboured to prove that their deities could do such and such things; "but Moses," writes Longinus, "no common-place man, when he would describe his God, contented himself with saying, 'God said, Let there be light; and there was light.'"

What rightly-directed mind cannot but be struck with amazement at the sublimity, the majesty of the opening sentence of the Pentateuch of Moses, in which against all the doctrines of chance, and such like wretched theories, Moses ascribes to God the creation of His own Universe? "In the beginning GOD created the Heavens and the Earth."

In reference to the Deluge we have two remarkable accounts by heathen authors, which we shall give for those of our readers who may not have access to these writings, and to whom the accounts may prove interesting. Ovid, who wrote immediately before and during the first twenty years of the Christian Era, gives a very full account of Creation, and of the first and happy, and then of the fallen and degenerate, state of man; and thus introduces the sad history of the sin of man, which caused Jupiter to destroy the earth by the flood:—

"Last of all came the Iron Age. Forthwith all manner of wickedness burst in upon the world. Modesty, truth, and good faith took flight; in their place came fraud, deceit, and treacherous lying in wait, and violence, and the cursed love of gain."

Ovid then describes the mode in which the very bowels of the earth were searched for especially the iron and the gold, the fruits of which search he thus describes: "And now the destructive iron, and the gold more injurious far, came forth. War making use of both stalks abroad, and with bloody hand brandishes the dreadful arms; men live on plunder; the host is not safe from his guest; nor the father-in-law from the son-in-law. Love of a brother is a rare thing. The husband plots the murder of the wife, and the wife that of the husband; fiendish stepmothers mix the lurid poison; and the son inquires before the time the age of his father. Piety lies prostrate; and the virgin goddess of justice, the last that remained of the heavenly visitors, abandoned the earth now drenched with blood."

What a resemblance to not only the account of Moses, but to that given by Isaiah (chap. lix.), especially where he says,—" And judgment is turned away backward, and justice standeth afar off; for truth is fallen in the street, and equity cannot enter." Well, we further read, that when Jupiter from the lofty citadel of heaven beheld this state of things he groaned, and called a council of the gods, and laid before them this desperate state of things; and then gives the dread sentence,—"I must now destroy the race of man over the whole surface of the earth; I swear by the Styx that all that could be done by me has been done; but the wound is incurable, and must be cut off by the sword." Jupiter further states, that he had himself gone down from heaven, and travelled about in human form, to see if the state of things was equal to the cry which reached his ear, but he found the evil report far less than the reality. Then Ovid proceeds to describe the manner in which the elements were collected for the work of destruction, when at last orders were given to open the doors and windows of heaven to co-operate with the waters below, and sweep an incurably guilty race from the face of the earth. "And now," continues Ovid, "sea and land had no longer any distinguishing feature; all was sea, and the sea had no shore." He then describes the vain efforts of men, animals, and birds, to save themselves; and then shows that only one spot was reserved as a resting-place for the little ark in which Deucalion and his wife were preserved; and in speaking of them he bears this testimony, "than whom was no better man, nor a greater lover of justice; nor any woman a more pious worshipper of the gods than she was."

The other account to which we have referred is by Lucian. He makes Timon rail at Jupiter in the most noisy and irreverent manner; so much so, that Timon thought he was a little too hard on celestial Jove; so he thus softens down the charge: "But that I may not speak too reproachfully, I admit, that then, when you had the vigour of youth, and especially in the time of the wickedness which caused the Flood, then you did act in a worthy manner against the villains—the hail came down like rocks; the rain was impetuous and violent—every drop a river. So much so, that in the time of Deucalion, such a wreck of nature occurred in a moment, that all things having been sunk under water were destroyed; so that one little ark was saved with difficulty, which rested on Lycores, preserving a mere spark of human life for the propagation of greater wickedness." For the propagation of greater wickedness! What a comment on "Why should ye be stricken any more? Ye will revolt yet more and more. The whole head is sick, the whole heart is faint."

Though not the immediate point before us, it may

amuse the reader to learn the way in which Jupiter received this noisy tirade of Timon; showing not only the wit of Lucian, but his opinion of the omniscience of Jove, and of the wisdom and piety of " the philosophers" of his day. " I say, Mercury, who is that fellow that is bawling at such a rate from Attica, near Hymettus, towards the foot of the mountain; a beggarly, dirty-looking fellow, clad in a goat's-skin jerkin? The fellow is stooping down as if he were digging: a very talkative fellow, with a large share of self-confidence. He must be a philosopher; or he would not otherwise have the audacity to utter such impious speech against us."

Moses then did not invent, but merely wrote the history of an article of belief which was universally received in the world. Moses however did more. He wrote his history as the true account of Creation, of the Fall of Man, and of the Deluge; and he wrote, as guided by and in the name, sometimes in the very words, of the Living and True GOD. This is the simple state of the case; and the question is,—Whether Moses or Bishop Colenso be the more credible witness on this subject; or, in other words, whether Moses is to be accounted a fool and deceiver, because Bishop Colenso, since his departure from England, made such advance in some of the sciences, in Geology in particular, as taught him his famous fact, which proved to his mind that the Mosaic account is pure fable.

This is the question,—Whether Moses was a mere fool, who took all things on trust, as he found the incidents, like fragments of wrecks on the waters of time,—" tanquam naufragii tabulæ;" and Bishop Colenso such a philosopher as to entitle him to sit in judgment on the wisdom and veracity of Moses. In fine,—Whether Moses was a retailer of falsehood, and

Bishop Colenso such a friend of truth, that *he* dared not shrink from repelling the lie, and placing it on the head of Moses, the time-honoured servant of God.

CHAPTER VI.

Character of Moses—His wisdom, greatness, and goodness—His an immortal name that will outlive all his calumniators—The Philosophy of Moses—Inconsistency of Bishop Colenso in retaining his office and its emoluments—Curious way in which a Pope dealt with a refractory Bishop—Moses' account of light—Of the blood, denied for a long time by Philosophers—Presented greater difficulties than the little calculations of Bishop Colenso—Moses found right on those points—Testimonies to the learning and wisdom of Moses—The Egyptians—The Motto on their Libraries —Moses' Code of Laws—The Pentateuch read every Sabbath—Witness of Christ to Moses.

IN treating the character of Moses we may, we think, assume without fear of contradiction that Moses was one of the greatest, wisest, and best men that ever lived. His name shall endure for ever in the annals of time. And in the unfading realms of light, truth, and glory, mention will be made of his honoured work. That eye which was not dim, and that natural force which was not abated, when his spirit took its flight from a world hastening to decay, has not yet set in darkness. Though long dead, he yet speaketh. He has survived the attacks of infidels of every class, and every clime, many of them men who could have taught philosophy to Bishop Colenso. And in spite of the Bishop's cavils and advance in some of the sciences since he left England,—and of his so great regard for truth, which compelled him in a moment of ridiculous folly to come before the public and proclaim the writings of Moses a fable, and Moses himself a liar—Moses and the writings which bear his name shall survive the cavils and carpings of infidel and little minds, when the tongues of his calumniators shall be silent in the grave; and the men who, against the happiness and honour of human nature, have so employed their wretched tongues and pens, if at all remembered, shall have passed into utter insignificance and contempt.

Moses delivered to mankind philosophy which modern ages have only begun to discover, and until such modern discoveries,—which, after all, are due not so much to human wisdom as to the inevitable knowledge of facts, which, as it rolls on, Time unfolds and forces on even the most indolent minds,—contracted and self-sufficient men were accustomed to act after the fashion now set us by a Christian Bishop, and throw their filthy but harmless mud at Moses, as if he had been created and endowed with such surpassing intellect and wisdom only to be in all ages the butt of shallow-pated fools.

The fashion now set us by a Christian Bishop, and in the full enjoyment of the emoluments of his office!—emoluments larger by many times than what would be accounted wealth by a vast body of the Clergy who follow the example of their Lord and Master, and really do His work; or by laymen of great minds and extensive knowledge who toil without ceasing for their daily support, as inheritors of, after all, the merciful part of the curse on our race, "In the sweat of thy face shalt thou eat bread until thou return unto the ground."

When we write thus, as we are compelled to do, of a Bishop, we, though certainly not a friend to Popery, have had the desire to be a Pope flash across our mind, that we might deal with this Bishop as he so richly deserves. In times gone by, when the Pope was master of England, and the Sovereign his lawgiver or executioner as suited the occasion, a Bishop of Oxford very much displeased the Pope; and though quite willing to trample on the laws of God, or of the country, the Pope could not entertain the impious thought of offering the least violence to the law ecclesiastical. He was therefore much perplexed as to the way of dealing with the refractory Bishop. At last he hit upon this plan; he resolved to promote him, an honour which the Bishop could not gainsay. So the Pope promoted the Bishop to a new see "in partibus infidelium," an imaginary see somewhere in the wilds of Africa, the exact locality of which the best geographer would have failed to discover, and where, our authority remarks, "the Bishop was like to starve for aught that his diocese afforded him."

Now this is just the way in which Bishop Colenso should be served, and permitted to live on his own property, or to earn his bread in an honest way by the resources of his mind; but not be allowed to exist, a living scandal, on money paid by Christians for the promotion of that period when "the earth shall be full of the knowledge of the LORD," without any exception of that written by Moses, "as the waters cover the sea." But to return to our argument.

Moses was for centuries multiplied by centuries an object of scorn in the writings of those wise men, wise at least in their own conceits, until time discovered the truth of his philosophy. "What an ignorant fool!" cried out one class of the philosophers; "why, he actually speaks of light as having been created some days before the sun, when WE know that the sun gives us light." "And how simple he was," cried another, "to afterwards contradict himself by stating that the sun was created to give light upon the earth, and to rule over the day."

Well; Moses did so write, and long afterwards the inspired Psalmist, in ascribing glory to God, refers to this account by Moses, and exclaims, "Thou hast created the light, and the sun."

It is not necessary now to discuss this question, which so long proved a far greater difficulty and ground of objection to the Mosaic history, than the petty arithmetical calculations of Bishop Colenso could possibly present. But it so happened that Moses was right; and if his revilers had possessed the least portion of the spirit of the great Newton, who, in the meridian splendour of his fame, felt himself as only a little child gathering pebbles on the shore of nature, they would not have been so forward to have proclaimed Moses a fool, and his writings a fable, or to have sought to establish their poor philosophy, not merely on the ruins of the wisdom and veracity of Moses, but on the ruins of philosophy itself.

"What a fool!" cried out another set of philosophers; "he says, 'The blood is the life.' Was ever greater nonsense published, when WE know that the life is in the brain?" cried one class. "In some other part of the body," cried another class of them. And though the body was a very small sphere for discovery of their theories, they could not agree among themselves as to the seat of life, yet they all knew a fact, which made them unanimous in crying down Moses as a fool. In this they all agreed, because Moses wrote such folly and fable as "The blood is the life."

We cannot now examine the passages in the other sacred books which assume the truth of the philosophy laid down by Moses on this subject. Of profane authors, Virgil has a passage which has always led us to suppose that he had some idea of the philosophy of life. And we have met, we think, passages in other heathen writers which show traces, though perhaps faint ones, of this idea, but it is not our purpose now to seek them out. Suffice it to say, that in this matter, too, Moses stated the truth, the philosophy of the question, which like many things in nature was suffered to lie hidden for ages; and, during such period of its having been so hidden, Moses had to bear the scorn and insults of self-styled philosophers, who, like Bishop Colenso, knew for certain a fact, which proved the Mosaic theory a fable, and its author a fool and deceiver of the human race.

But one day the truth burst in like a flood of light on the mind of Hunter, while he was engaged, not in seeking to reconcile Moses with truth, or philosophy with Moses, or in thinking of Moses at all, but while merely engaged in the study of his profession. And Hunter demonstrated to the world, that "the blood is the life," the living circulating principle.

And now, if we could imagine an assembly in one of the great halls of London wholly composed of infidels, and Satan himself,—the father of lies and the accuser of Moses and the brethren,—in the chair, not one man, with the least pretensions to knowledge, could be found possessed of courage to stand up even in such a constituted assembly and deny this fact, or charge Moses with folly and falsehood for having so many thousand years ago made the statement, "The blood is the life."

And thus, as Moses, in respect to this point also, has outlived the attacks of our "philosophers," so we think that he will outlive the short term of the five years granted by Bishop Colenso to the Church of England, to be forsaken by the people if the Church do not agree with the Bishop in proclaiming the Pentateuch of Moses a fable and a lie.

We might bring forward other points on which the philosophers of Bishop Colenso's School and Moses have been at variance; and on which it also so happened that Moses either wrote the truth, or did not write such inconsistency with truth or true philosophy as those men, so puffed up with the idea of their own wisdom, have ascribed to him. But let us turn to another view of the question.

We shall now glance at some of the testimonies to the learning and wisdom of Moses.

It is a fine remark of Sallust, that, considering the nature and shortness of human life, our desire and aim should be to make the remembrance of ourselves, "memoriam nostrî," as lasting as possible. But according to the conceit of the ancients, to which Lord Bacon refers, all men when dying had small medals with their names and actions hung around their necks; and as their shades were being carried across the river Lethe, the medals of most men fell into that river, where all things were forgotten. But around some few certain birds hovered, which caught up the falling medals and carried them into the region of life and immortality.

Whatever has become of the medals of the host of calumniators of Moses we shall not waste time in inquiring. But of one thing we are not left in doubt, that Moses lives, and shows not any symptom of decay. Fifteen hundred years after his departure from this world the first Christian martyr, when tracing from the writings of Moses the dealings of God with man, thus spake:

"Now Moses was learned in all the wisdom of the Egyptians, and was mighty in words and in deeds."

We do not propose to give even a sketch of that great nation, the ancient Egyptians. Suffice it to say that a greater compliment or honour could not have been bestowed on any man. But we may notice one idea of theirs worthy of their greatness. It was their custom to inscribe over the doors of their libraries, "The medicine of the soul." A noble sentiment! showing that true knowledge is not to be obtained by looking at books, or by consulting the index, or by "reading by the margin," but by its being taken into the soul as medicine is into the body, so as, in the same manner that medicine does, to become one with, part and parcel of, the soul.

On this idea our beautiful Collect gives a good commentary, when we pray that we may so "hear, read, mark, learn, and inwardly digest" the words of the Holy Scriptures, that we may thereby "embrace and ever hold fast the blessed hope of everlasting life," to confer which those sacred writings were delivered to man.

Now this is an idea in reference to which our modern professors of flippancy would do well to imitate the wise example of the ancient Egyptians, and learn at least their own ignorance, before they volunteer to carp and cavil at the productions of great minds.

Moses has left behind him in his writings a name, which, as it has survived the marble and brass that have been in countless instances employed, and employed in vain, to perpetuate the memory of men who left not any thing untried to force themselves on posterity, will survive, when all the generations who have trod this earth shall have passed with earth itself into their original nothingness. His code of laws has not only immortalized his name, but also the names of men who, by consent of mankind, have been entitled great because of their having had the greatness to base their laws on the code of that great lawgiver.

His Pentateuch, that fable of Bishop Colenso, was publicly read from his own day down to the Christian era. At the first—the Apostolic—council of the Christian Church it was recorded:—"For Moses of old time hath in every city them that preach him, being read in the synagogues every sabbath day." Nay, his countrymen were ordered to engrave his writings on their door-posts, and also on the borders of their garments, and to teach them to their children on all occasions.

And from the Christian era to the present hour, the name and writings of Moses, that forger of lies in the name of the Lord, have travelled hand in hand with the name of the Redeemer Himself, so that it might, in a sense, be said of him, "Then I said, It is a light thing that thou shouldest be My servant to raise up the tribes of Jacob, and to restore the preserved of Israel. I will also give thee to be a light of the Gentiles, that thou mayest be My salvation unto the ends of the earth."

By the "fable" of Moses the Lord Jesus convicted the Sadducees who denied the resurrection, by the words which God spake by Moses out of the midst of the bush,—"I am the God of Abraham, and the God of Isaac, and the God of Jacob."

And by the testimony of the writer of the Pentateuch the Saviour proved His own mission, by showing that the proof of His mission and the writings of Moses must stand or fall together. "Think not that I will accuse you unto the Father. There is one that accuseth you, even Moses, in whom ye trust. For had ye believed Moses, ye would have believed Me; for he wrote of Me. But if ye believe not his writings, how can ye believe My words?"

CHAPTER VII.

Personal character of Moses—Piety and nobility of mind exhibited by Moses—Offer made him—Selected by God as the man who only could have turned away His wrath—Appointed to appear at the Transfiguration—Moses' name remembered in Heaven—Moses the man whom Bishop Colenso charges with folly and falsehood—The great scandal of the Bishop's conduct—Way in which the Bishop disposes of all testimony, even that of the whole Scriptures and of Christ Himself—The Mission of Christ to publish truth and warn against error—According to Bishop Colenso that Mission a failure—Sin of speaking for God where He has not spoken—This the crowning guilt of the Papacy—Bishop Colenso would represent Christ as encouraging such sin—Impiety as well as vanity of such mode of argument.

As to the piety, absence of selfishness, and nobility of mind, which the life of Moses exhibits, language itself would fail to do him justice. Let this one instance speak. When such an offer was made to Moses, as before or since was never made to man, he appeared as if he never heard the words in which it was conveyed, and why? He wholly forgot himself, and never bestowed a thought on the dazzling glory presented to his mind, because the honour of his Creator and Master was at stake.

"And the LORD said unto Moses, How long will this people provoke Me? and how long will it be ere they believe Me, for all the signs which I have showed among them? I will smite them with the pestilence, and disinherit them, and will make of thee a greater nation and mightier than they. And Moses said unto the Lord, Then the Egyptians shall hear it, (for Thou broughtest up this people in Thy might from among them;) and they will tell it to the inhabitants of this land: for they have heard that Thou LORD art among this people, that Thou LORD art seen face to face, and that Thy cloud standeth over them, and that Thou goest before them, by day time in a pillar of a cloud, and in a pillar of fire by night. Now if Thou shalt kill all this people as one man, then the nations which have heard the fame of Thee will speak, saying, Because the LORD was not able to bring this people into the land which He sware unto them, therefore He hath slain them in the wilderness. And now, I beseech Thee, let the power of my LORD be great, according as Thou hast spoken, saying, The LORD is longsuffering, and of great mercy, forgiving iniquity and transgression, and by no means clearing the guilty, visiting the iniquity of the fathers upon the children unto the third and fourth *generation*. Pardon, I beseech Thee, the iniquity of this people according unto the greatness of Thy mercy, and as Thou hast forgiven this people, from Egypt even until now."

To add one word of comment to this speech and prayer, would be to destroy the force of one of the most noble specimens of writing ever recorded.

This was the man whom the Almighty selected by name, to show that if any individual of the human race could have turned away His anger from a wicked generation, Moses would have been the man. "Then said the LORD unto me, Though Moses and Samuel stood before Me, yet My mind could not be toward this people."

This, too, was the man appointed by Heaven to appear in company with Elias at the transfiguration of the Lord of life and glory. And this is the man whose name shall be heard throughout all ages in the realms of glory (for, in spite of the philosophy of Bishop Colenso, we assume the truth of the Holy Scriptures), in concert with that of the Redeemer Himself, as often as the heavenly choir chant "the song of Moses and of the Lamb."

And this is the man whom Doctor Colenso, a Christian Bishop, has dared to blaspheme; whom in his self-conceit this Bishop of Natal has stigmatized as an inventor of fables, and wilful deceiver of mankind; as one who wrote lies, and wrote them in the name and alleged words of that High and Lofty One that inhabiteth eternity, whose Omnipotence is restrained by one, only one, thing, that He cannot lie,—" GOD that cannot lie."

If, we once more say, an avowed "fool," one who would openly say, " I do not believe in a God;" or a fool of another class who would say,—" I believe in God, but I will not believe that He could, or, if He could, that He would, make a revelation of Himself to His creatures," though God has made a revelation of Himself in the Book of Nature, which infidels cannot deny; if such men were to act thus,—as men of such avowed opinions have in all ages acted,—reason is that we might bear with them, for we cannot gather grapes of thorns, or figs of thistles; but that a Bishop of the Church of Christ, and in full enjoyment of the position and revenues of his high and sacred office, should volunteer to thus come forward and blaspheme such a man as Moses, to whom and to whose writings such commanding and unqualified testimony has been borne; this—this is a disgrace and reproach not only to the Bishop himself, but to the Church and Nation that could tolerate such a crying scandal.

" Pudet hæc opprobria nobis
Et dici potuisse; et non potuisse refelli."

We need not, however, wonder at this, when we consider that Bishop Colenso, instead of bringing, as he promised and vowed, every thought into subjection to Christ, has advanced the "one step left above them all," and has impeached and insulted the word of the Redeemer Himself.

The Bishop quotes some of the passages above cited, in which Christ bears testimony to the character and writings of Moses; but of all this positive evidence, and from such authority, Bishop Colenso disposes in this very easy way: that as the Redeemer was very man, and was said to have increased in wisdom, He had not any more knowledge of such questions as the truth of the Pentateuch, than any other Jew of the day might have had; that, in fact, the Saviour took on trust the traditionary testimony to the credibility of the Pentateuch, which the wisdom and "fact" of Bishop Colenso now prove to the world is, after all, a mere fable — a lie "spoken in the name of the Lord."

This is the way in which the Bishop of Natal speaks of Him who knew the thoughts of man, who needed not that any should testify of man, for He knew what was in man; of Him who, unless the Bible be no better than the fable of Mahomet, was "the Lord from heaven;" and who, though He charged the Jews with having made void the word of God, the Old Testament, by their traditions, never once charged them even in the least degree with having added thereto or taken therefrom. Such is the way in which Bishop Colenso speaks of Him, who came to deliver truth to man, and who referred to the Books of Moses, as we have above set forth, as writings which must stand or fall with the truth of His own mission and His own words, the words of Him "in whom are hid all the treasures of wisdom and knowledge;" of whom His enemies in all ages have confessed "never man spake like this man;" and who in these words delivered the final judgment against the appeal of the rich man in hell to have a miracle wrought to convince his brethren lest they also should come down to his gloomy abode, "If they believe not Moses and the Prophets, neither will they be persuaded though one rose from the dead."

"But all this testimony must go to the idle winds, and my testimony must stand, that the Pentateuch of Moses is a mere fable; and it must be a fable because I, Bishop Colenso, know for certain a fact; and I know that fact because since my departure from England I made much advance in some of the sciences, in geology in particular."

This is the sum and substance of Bishop Colenso's *reasoning*, and yet the Bishop is reported to be a mathematician! This easy mode of avoiding truth, and disposing of the testimony of the Saviour, reminds us of an instance, given in the masterly work on the Atonement by Archbishop Magee, of the way in which Priestly dealt with a passage of Holy Writ which much perplexed the Socinian School.

"I never yet," says Priestly, (we quote from memory, but we give the substance accurately,) "met with a satisfactory explanation of this verse from any of our body, 'And no man hath ascended up to heaven; but He that came down from heaven, even the Son of Man which is in heaven.' But sooner than admit the absurdity (that was, in his eyes, the deity of Christ), he would resort to the old Socinian notion, that Christ after His birth was taken up into heaven to be instructed as a teacher, and sent down again, or that the Apostle was old when he wrote the words (or, in plain language, doting), or that he dictated one thing, and his amanuensis wrote another."

This is certainly a most easy and convenient mode of disposing of the Word of God, when any part thereof may not suit our own notions. And this is the very way in which Bishop Colenso deals with the sacred writings, and with the words of the Redeemer Himself, when those writings and words do not square with the petty notions of his mind.

The mission of the Lord Jesus Christ was to publish the truth, and to warn mankind against error and falsehood of every kind. But Christ not only did not warn men against errors in the Pentateuch; He did not say, "Do not lay any stress on My quotations or references or testimonies to Moses; for while I thus refer, quote, and testify, I warn the race of man against all those foolish fables in the account of the Deluge, and many other parts of that foolish work;" but He gave to Moses, and Moses' writings, unqualified testimony, as we have now proved; whereas, if the wisdom of Bishop Colenso were to take the place of the Revelation of God, the Saviour should have rebuked Moses, and with the greatest severity, for writing fables and speaking lies; and especially for the daring impiety of sending forth those fables and lies as if they were the truth—the very words of the Almighty. For of what more daring impiety could any creature be guilty?

What, for instance, is the crowning sin of the Papacy? Not—though so bad—the mere teaching of transubstantiation, purgatory, saint-worship, image-worship, and the other false doctrines, heresies, and schisms of her new creed,—but her daring and blasphemous presumption in usurping the name and prerogative of Almighty God, and publishing to His creatures, and in His Name, and as His truth, a new religion, and enforcing the same on the consciences of men, as conditions of Christian communion and salvation, under pain of the heaviest penalties in this life, and of eternal damnation in the life beyond the grave.

To represent, then, the blessed Redeemer as giving His sanction and positive testimony to such wickedness,—for this is the only light in which the argument of Bishop Colenso, when properly examined, can be viewed,—this is indeed a new kind of impiety, and taught by a Christian Bishop! which is revolting to the mind of any man who has the least knowledge of himself or of his Creator.

"I grant you," writes this Christian Bishop, "that Christ did thus quote and refer to, and testify of Moses; but even He, the Christ, the Son of the living God, knew no more of the matter than did any Jew of the day." He took all this on trust, and as none of the Jews of that day, or before or since that day, and also as none of the men who have lived in Christian times had the knowledge and advance in some of the sciences of which the Bishop of Natal can boast, then we are not to place any reliance on one or all of them; no, not even on the testimony of Christ Himself, though He was "the Lord from heaven." And therefore, to conclude all, Bishop Colenso was and is right in proclaiming the writings of Moses a mere fable, and Moses himself a deceiver,—a wilful deceiver,—who was not afraid to pass off his fables as truth, and as truth spoken in the name and words of the LORD.

CHAPTER VIII.

Not bound to answer objections of Bishop Colenso—His fallacy of reasoning from such objections—The remark of Origen adopted and improved on by Butler—Those objections do not furnish any ground for the conclusion of Bishop Colenso—The Bishop's remarks respecting the Pentateuch and Inspiration—The testimony of the Redeemer that the words of Moses and of God are one and the same—The Saviour's definition of Inspiration—The vanity of Bishop Colenso in supposing that men of past ages never examined the grounds of belief—The superior vigour and learning of former ages.

WE are not bound to examine, with a view to their solution, the objections which Bishop Colenso brings forward as the lever by which he would overturn the Christian religion,—we say the Christian religion,—for in spite of all professions to the contrary, from whatever motive pleaded, his work at least endeavours to overthrow Christianity, and to substitute mere deism in its place. We have abundantly proved in former chapters the fallacy of his mode of reasoning from difficulties, objections, and cavils against writings sustained by an overwhelming weight of positive evidence; the rejection of which would convert the history of the world into an idle tale, and put a bar in the way of all belief.

We shall, however, touch on those objections; but only to discuss them in the way which we have laid down, to show that those difficulties, even if we admit them to be such, do not furnish any ground to justify the pretensions of Bishop Colenso to impeach the varacity of Moses by denouncing his writings as a fable and a lie.

Even far greater grounds of objection, founded on

our ignorance or inability to comprehend all the mysteries and difficulties in the economy of our Maker, would not justify such a very illogical conclusion as that to which Bishop Colenso would lead us, that the works in which those mysteries and difficulties are found must be mere fable and falsehood.

There is true wisdom in the remark of Origen, on which Bishop Butler has founded his immortal work, "That he who believes the Scripture to have proceeded from Him who is the Author of Nature, may well expect to find the same sort of difficulties in it, as are found in the constitution of Nature." On which remark Butler thus so well improves, "And in a like way of reflection it may be added, that he who denies the Scripture to have been from God upon account of these difficulties, may, for the very same reason, deny the world to have been formed by Him."

The Almighty Ruler of the Universe unfolds from age to age many things that are true and of the greatest value, and that were hidden for centuries from the greatest minds, and only discovered when in the exercise of His Providence He made them plain. But, even while thus hidden, he would not have been accounted a very wise man who would have made those difficulties, and his inability to comprehend and explain them, from whatever cause that inability may have proceeded, a ground for denouncing the book of nature as a fable and a lie.

What a pity that, before he so exposed himself, Bishop Colenso did not ask his own mind the question:—"Has the Creator endowed me above all men with such infallible means of arriving at the knowledge and truth of all questions, that I can understand and solve all mysteries and difficulties in the works of nature and grace, so that what I say must rule the world?"

We shall then only examine the cavils of Bishop Colenso to prove how very little ground they furnish for such assumption on his part of that superior wisdom and veracity which he is not indulgent enough to concede to Moses, or, indeed, even to the Redeemer Himself, who said, "I am the light of the world."

In the first section of his introductory remarks to his objections, the Bishop gives a definition of the word Pentateuch, as also a sketch of its history as ascribed to Moses by general belief, and of the way in which Moses may have obtained his information. "It is believed," the Bishop writes, "he (Moses) was under such constant control and superintendence of the Spirit of God that he was kept from any serious error, and certainly from writing any thing altogether untrue." "It is believed," that is, such is the statement usually made—made by men of weak minds—but which we philosophers who know any thing of science must reject as absurd and untrue.

There was not any necessity for all the Bishop's writing and quotations to give any explanation of inspiration. The matter is very simple. It is a mere question of truth or falsehood. Moses states that he wrote by command of God, as instructed by God, and in many places he records words as the very words and commands of God. And Moses was not excepted by the Apostle, when he said, "Holy men of God spake as they were moved by the Holy Ghost." And Christ Himself confirms the claim of Moses to have written by express command of God, by making the words written by Moses one and the same as the words of God.

"But as touching the resurrection of the dead, have ye not read that which was spoken unto you by God, saying, I am the God of Abraham, and the God of Isaac, and the God of Jacob?" Again; "And as touching the dead, that they rise; have ye not read in the book of Moses, how in the bush God spake unto him, saying," &c.? There is not therefore any need of arguments or quotations. The question is, we say, a mere matter of fact,—Which is the more credible? Bishop Colenso, who charges on Moses the sin of writing folly and falsehood in the name, and as the truth of God; or Moses, who says that he did write in the name of God, by the command of God, and the very words of God; or Christ Himself, who has set His seal to the testimony of Moses on this very question?

If it were our present business to discuss the position, how the Eternal Spirit acts on the human mind, or to give any positive instruction on this subject to believers in the inspired Volume, we might produce much and profitable matter. But such is not our point; nor is it the way to answer Bishop Colenso, or such a specimen of vanity and science, falsely so called, as his book displays.

We content ourselves with this observation,—that the best mode of arriving at some idea of this question (for, after all, what can we know of such a lofty subject in our present imperfect condition?) is to give the words of our Lord, to show the way in which the Holy Spirit may have influenced the inspired writers in days before His coming, by the way in which the same Spirit was to influence the Apostles of the Christian Church:—"Howbeit when He, the Spirit of truth, is come, He will guide you into all truth; for He shall not speak of Himself; but whatsoever He shall hear, that shall He speak: and He will show you things to come."

Our Almighty Creator, who wills the happiness of His creatures, and who published His glorious Revelation to give them light and joy in this dark vale of tears,—who, in His own words, makes them "rejoice from their sorrow,"—can select, in the exercise of that Providence which "ordereth all things both in heaven and in earth," any instruments to promote His benevolent and merciful ends. He not only ordains the end, but appoints also the means by which that end is attained. He may choose, as He has done, an Isaiah, or a Jeremiah, or a St. John, or a Saul of Tarsus; and leave each without any constraint to pursue his own style; and yet guard one and all of such instruments from writing any thing but truth—and His truth. And so with respect to the writings of Moses, to which, independently of other testimony, the Lord Jesus Christ has set His seal that they are the truth— the very words of God; but which, notwithstanding all this evidence, Bishop Colenso has discovered and proved to be a fable!

In his next paragraph the Bishop writes,—"But among the many results of that remarkable activity, in scientific inquiry of every kind, which, by God's own gift, distinguishes the present age, this must also be reckoned, that attention and labour are now being bestowed, more closely than ever before, to search into the real foundations for such a belief as this."

Now, we very humbly hope that, if our volume should reach Bishop Colenso or any disciples of his School, they will not be displeased if we say, that all this is most wretched boasting in the eyes of any one who has read the productions of great minds, and of great minds of ages long past. It is an astonishing display of vanity on the part of Bishop Colenso, and his guides and followers, to imagine that they are the only wise men; that wisdom was born or will die with them; and that the age which produced them is the only age that ever made any advance in science, or "any search into the real foundations for such a belief as this."

This is mere "learned nonsense," or "learned ignorance;" we do not now remember which of those terms is used by Locke to expose such affectation of learning. The reading of any man must have been wonderfully contracted who can persuade himself that this is *the* age, and that the great men of former times were fools, or that they never made any search into those points which, as Bishop Colenso thinks, escaped the notice of other men.

We must, however, confess that we have found one original objection to the Pentateuch in the book of Bishop Colenso. But as we do not desire to enter on that original idea of the Bishop, either to deprive him of the merit so justly due to him for having thought of such a point, or to discuss such a very peculiar question, we shall not bestow more notice on the subject than to express our wonder that Bishop Colenso should have made the truth of the Revelation of God to man to depend on his difficulty as to how a large encampment of human beings were to find means for relieving the "common necessities of nature!" Oh! Bishop Colenso! Bishop Colenso! "O tempora! O mores!"

But to pass by this, so far as we have ever read, most original argument against the truth of the writings of Moses, we say, that the study of the works of former days have given a distaste for modern productions, and especially for the productions of too many of our philosophers of the nineteenth century. There was, as has been observed, a smell of the lamp about the works of men of former ages, which is not to be found in every writer of the present day.

We have great men now, and they are men who are not forward on every occasion to make a loud noise to attract attention; but still we believe what we have said as to the writings of men of days now numbered with "the years beyond the flood," and we state our belief with the view of giving such boasting philosophers a hint not to be so overwise in their own ignorant conceit, as to conclude that there have not existed in the world as deep and able critics as Bishop Colenso and his "brave souls who yearn for light, and battle for the truth."

CHAPTER IX.

Further notice of the Animals in the Ark—The design of God in this —No greater difficulty than the bestowal of instinct—No more difficulty to God in sustaining them than in the way in which He provides for such a variety of creatures—The wonderful instinct of animals an argument of the wisdom and power of God —The Almighty not to be called to account by man—Supposed case of a man for the first time seeing the difficulties in the world—The conclusion to which Bishop Colenso would drive such a man—The rod of Moses—The ass of Balaam—Admitted folly of such things possible apart from the interference of God —No room for arithmetic here—Slavery—"His money"—The Quixotic attack on Moses for use of the words—Moses did not establish Slavery—Laid down just laws for all classes.

WE have already noticed, though merely noticed, the great point of Bishop Colenso, the impossibility of animals congregating and entering into the ark for the preservation of their lives from the approaching ruin of earth. This was the stone of stumbling to the untaught Zulu, whose very natural doubts the Bishop answered in the way described in former chapters. This point, too, furnished the Bishop one unanswerable argument against the truth of the Mosaic history, and in favour of his conclusion that the whole account is fable, and lies spoken in the name of the Lord.

In our quotation from Ovid we have seen the description, founded on tradition, of the fruitless efforts of all not shut up in the ark to rescue themselves from the fury of the waters of heaven and earth when met in concord to overwhelm this lower world. Moses states that the Creator, designing to keep some alive, did by the actings of His Providence cause them to take refuge in the ark, to be saved from the universal destruction, and to be kept alive for the use of earth and its inhabitants who were to survive the deluge, and to be links in the great chain of His plan of transmitting to all future generations the proof of His faithfulness, Who, when building the pillar to set forth His power, justice, and glory, crowns it with, "Who keepeth His promise for ever."

We have shown that the endowment of the mere animal creation, beasts, birds, and fishes, with the astonishing instinct which they possess is as great a wonder, if carefully examined, as would be their flocking to the ark under the guidance of His Providence. With the one we are so familiar that we never bestow a thought on the subject. The other is of course contrary to common experience. We need not go into any question of the size of the ark, or of the difficulty of bringing the animals into or of supporting them in the same. To the Creator the one is as easy as the other. His greatness and wisdom are as much displayed in gilding the wing of the butterfly, as in the regulation of the innumerable orbs which stud the firmament.

Pliny was amazed at the "stupendous littleness" of a gnat, as a proof of the greatness of the Creator. What would have been his wonder had he known the microscope, and by it have seen the multitude of creatures that find a dwelling in a drop of water? There could not then be in the nature of the thing any derogation from His greatness on the part of the Creator in an arrangement to keep alive the works of

His hands; and for His own purposes, purposes of which we now can see so little. The bestowal of the instinct was as great an exercise of His power and wisdom, as the acting on that instinct in order to preserve seed of His creatures for carrying out of His plans then only in the womb of time.

And what greater difficulty to the Creator in sustaining them during the days that the windows of heaven were open, and the fountains and foundations of the earth were broken up, than in the astonishing, incredible if we did not see it, way in which Almighty God in His goodness now provides for the vast multitudes of beings that inhabit the earth, the sea, and the air? "Can God furnish a table in the wilderness?" "Can He give bread also?" was the cry of old, and may be the cry of "philosophers" of our own day. But to any well-regulated and reflecting mind it will be manifest that the way in which "Our Father, who is in Heaven," provides "daily bread," not merely for man, but for the endless variety of His creatures that people earth, sea, and sky, is a constant succession of wonders, nay, almost miracle upon miracle.

The very bread by which man is fed, the way in which it is produced, and in which it supports life, is as great a difficulty, if we exclude the interposition and appointment of the Creator, as the assembling and supporting of His creatures in the ark.

We do not propose a dissertation on this subject. Nor are we called on by the plan of our work, nor by any thing in the volume of Bishop Colenso, to give any solution of the difficulties in question, or of any difficulties in the book of nature or of the book of grace; as if we were obliged or were competent to explain the whole, or even the smallest part, of that amazing process by which the economy of the Creator is conducted; or as if we had the right or power to bring down that wisdom and understanding which are infinite to the level of our ignorance and folly. But it may profit some of our readers to have their attention called to those displays of the power and wisdom of God in things that, because of every-day occurrence, not only might, but actually do, escape the notice of too large a portion of the human race.

On the endowment of animal creatures with the instinct which they exhibit, and which could be the work of God alone, the learned Mr. Ray, already quoted, writes: that "it is a great argument of a superior Author of their and other natures, who hath endued them with these instincts, whereby they are as it were acted and driven to bring about ends which themselves aim not at (so far as we can discern), but are directed to; for (as Aristotle observes) 'they act not by art, neither do they inquire, neither do they deliberate about what they do.'

"And, therefore, as Dr. Cudworth saith well, they are not masters of that wisdom according to which they act, but only passive to the instincts and impresses thereof upon them. And indeed to affirm, that brute animals do all these things by a knowledge of their own, and which themselves are masters of, and that without deliberation and consultation, were to make them to be endued with a most perfect intellect, far transcending that of human reason; whereas it is plain enough that brutes are not above consultation, but below it, and that these instincts of nature in them are nothing but a kind of fate upon them.

"The migration of birds from an hotter to a colder country, or a colder to an hotter, according to the seasons of the year, as their nature is, I know not how to give an account of, it is so strange and admirable. What moves them to shift their quarters? You will say, the disagreeableness of the temper of the air to the constitution of their bodies, or want of food. But how come they to be directed to the same place yearly, though sometimes but a little island, the soland goose to the Bass of Edinburgh Frith, which they could not possibly see, and so it could have no influence upon them that way? The cold or the heat might possibly drive them in a right line from either; but that they should impel land-birds to venture over a wide ocean, of which they can see no end, is strange and unaccountable; one would think that the sight of so much water, and present fear of drowning, should overcome the sense of hunger, or disagreeableness of the temper of the air.

"Besides, how come they to steer their course aright to their several quarters, which before the compass was invented was hard for man himself to do, they being not able, as I noted before, to see them at that distance? Think we that the quails, for instance, could see quite across the Mediterranean sea? and yet it is clear they fly out of Italy into Africa, lighting many times on ships in the midst of the sea, to rest themselves when tired and spent with flying. That they should thus shift places, is very convenient for them, and accordingly we see they do it: which seems to be impossible they should, unless themselves were endued with reason, or directed and acted by a superior intelligent cause."

Seeing then that "God is greater than man," and that He giveth not account of any of His matters, "Am I," any person with proper knowledge of himself, and with due reverence for his Maker, would say, "Am I to challenge the Most High because He has not discovered to me all His plans, and the windings of His ways, which are unsearchable and past finding out? and because I cannot see into those plans and ways which He has thus concealed from the range of my finite vision, am I to turn infidel, and insult and deny the truth, nay, the existence of the book of nature in which these difficulties are thus published?"

And yet these are only a small portion of the large collection of difficulties which the same book contains. And the book of nature not only records such difficulties, but we see them before our eyes every day. We therefore must admit though we cannot give any explanation of them, except the will of the Almighty. We at least cannot from their existence deny the truth of God speaking in the book of nature.

But if we imagine the case of a man brought into the world without any knowledge of those subjects, because without any experience of his own, and without the advantage of "standing on the shoulders of those who have gone before," and thus becoming "aged in a moment;" but yet such a man endued with a vigorous mind, and with all means for the exercise of its powers; then such a man might very naturally doubt on all those points involving the difficulties now named, and might, nay, must go even so far as to declare, on the principle laid down by Bishop Colenso, the whole book of nature a mere fable.

And on the same principle are we to blaspheme the God of grace, and deny the truth of His revelation, because we do not every day see a flood, an ark, and animals directed to it for shelter and for preservation of life? Is the one more impossible to the Creator than the other? more difficult for the exercise of His power, of which His pious servant said, "I know that Thou canst do all things?" And are we to go farther, and cavil at and deny the truth of His book of grace? And if we do, then, to be consistent, we must deny the truth of all writings, of every thing; because we do not know the way in which the Creator exercises

His Providence, and acts on the minds and instincts of His creatures. Of course, as we have before said, all these instances, the difficulties in the book of nature or in the book of grace, assume the interference of the Supreme Being, or else the discussion of the question for even a single moment would be only waste of time.

And are we to be turned from the path of wisdom—that "path which no fowl knoweth, and which the vulture's eye hath not seen," and which can be discovered to us only by the God of wisdom,—by such a mode of cavilling as that by which the author of the wretched work in question seeks to pervert the right ways of the Lord, and to turn men aside from the path of light and truth?

THE ROD OF MOSES AND THE ASS OF BALAAM.

The rod of Moses and the ass of Balaam have furnished in all ages many a scoff to infidels of every class. Bishop Colenso introduces these two incidents as part of a collection of points which help to make up his "fact," by which he proves the Pentateuch utterly destitute of truth. And while the Bishop enters largely into calculations as to population and the laws of increase, the food of animals, and the exact space into which a given number of the human race may be crowded,—or some such childish specimens of the powers of a certain class of philosophers,—the rod of Moses, and the ass that "speaking with man's voice forbad the madness of the prophet," he seems to dismiss with the contempt becoming a great mind; much like the way adopted by the great men of old, who would not condescend to even discuss the merits of the mission of Christ, but settled the question with "Can any thing good come out of Nazareth?"

Now does Bishop Colenso imagine that we are all fools,—or that Moses who wrote these matters was a fool,—to believe that, in the ordinary course of nature, a rod could become a serpent, or that an ass should speak with man's voice? There is not any room for arithmetic here. No plus or minus will explain or refute those two most extraordinary circumstances.

We shall not offer any explanation of such, nor shall we discuss the question of the difficulty; nor of the occasion, or the grand result of the confounding the sorcerers who lent themselves to practise and trade upon a people, who, though then the greatest nation on earth for wisdom and learning, were spell-bound by the most wicked, cruel, and debasing superstition and idolatry. To the peculiar belief and practices of that nation the plagues, and the means by which the mission of Moses was established, were especially adapted. The reader will find those points ably and unanswerably treated in the several works written on that part of the question.

To come then to our prescribed mode of examination of the superior wisdom and veracity of Bishop Colenso over that of the inspired writers, we say,—It is not necessary to prove the self-evident proposition, that a rod is not, and could not of itself become, a serpent, and that an ass could not speak; and that daily experience proves the truth of this position. The poor ass can only bray; and the bray is his prayer for food. For "doth the wild ass bray when he hath grass?" The bray is like the young lion's prayer described in the psalm, "The young lions roar after their prey, and seek their meat from God."

And does Bishop Colenso imagine that we are not as much startled as he can be at the idea of the "dumb ass speaking with man's voice?" And to pass away from ourselves to Moses, the vilified and grossly insulted servant of God, and to the Apostles of our Lord, who said that they did not follow "cunningly-devised fables," we wonder that it did not occur to Bishop Colenso, that, as Moses was one of the greatest of men, he must have known the utter absurdity of writing, that a dumb ass that by nature can only bray should speak with man's voice; and that his writing such a statement would furnish food, in all ages, for those scoffs and gibes, which are "wont to set the table in a roar." We might, by the way, ask such philosophers' empty skulls, "Where be your gibes now?"

Birds can be taught to speak, but the poor donkey can only bray. And Moses knew all this. It was not reserved for the nineteenth century to prove the contrary. And a man like Moses could not have written such statements if they had not been true. He would not have had the moral courage to have sent out such, if they had not happened; just as St. Paul never could have sent out his "We preach Christ crucified," in answer to the bigoted Jews and the philosophizing Greeks; or his "God forbid that I should glory, save in the Cross of our Lord Jesus Christ." To the natural mind the one is as great an absurdity and stumbling-block as the other, if we view the subject apart from the purposes and interposition of the Creator and Redeemer of the World.

With what different eyes men see! Numbers of our race, indeed an innumerable multitude of beings endowed with reason, have concluded the truth of all this from the fact of its having been recorded by a servant of God like Moses, who was also commissioned by God to deliver such striking prophecies, the fulfilment of which are before our eyes at this present day.

If we did not regard the Pentateuch as part of the Revelation of God, we should not discuss this question; so we do not require the wisdom or veracity of Bishop Colenso to teach us that, in the course of nature, an ass could not speak with man's voice. And yet the great and good and wise Moses so spake; and so it was believed by all the inspired writers down to the Apostle Peter, who wrote—" The dumb ass, speaking with man's voice, forbad the madness of the prophet." But all those men lived before the days of our modern philosophers!

THE SLAVE—" HIS MONEY."

There is in his preface only one more objection on which Bishop Colenso founds his charge against Moses as the writer of fables, with the notice of which we shall trouble ourselves or our readers. We refer to the question of slavery. The Bishop describes the horror of his Zulu and of himself when the words came before them—" For he is his money." Was that the first time that the Bishop ever read or heard of those words? We do not speak of the poor Zulu, for he did not know any thing of the Holy Scriptures; he was not born in a Christian land; was not educated at a Christian University; did not voluntarily enter into holy orders; was not a rector or vicar of a parish, or afterwards a Bishop; we, therefore, make every allowance for him.

But it does seem strange that a Bishop should have been, for the first time in his life, horror-struck with the words " for he is his money," and should have determined from that moment to go forth in the spirit of Don Quixote against the book in which such wickedness was proclaimed, and prove to all men of the present day, and for the benefit—indeed we suppose happiness—of " generations yet unborn," that the book, in which such a dreadful sentence is recorded, is not the revelation of God, but a mere medley of fable, folly, falsehood, and wrong. This is not a historical question; this is a question, in the Bishop's view of the Pentateuch, containing most fearfully cruel and otherwise wicked principles.

"Master, Master," said Sancho to Don Quixote, "they be but very sheep," when, having charged a windmill, the knight was about to attack the unoffending flock as enemies to the human race. But the poor Don, bent on the high resolve to root out all oppression from the earth, was not to be restrained by the remonstrance of Sancho. As he charged the windmill, so he charged the sheep. And he has left behind him an immortal name.

It appears to us as if the Bishop of Natal and the Zulu had changed places, and that, instead of teaching Christianity to the Zulu race, the Bishop was by them confirmed in—we will not say taught—infidelity. The only difference was, that the poor Zulu had not the office or emoluments of the See. We certainly do feel astonished at such incidents, which led to the attack by Bishop Colenso on the Inspired Volume, which was not guilty of any thing, so far as we can see, which could justify such determined—indeed malignant—enmity on the part of a Christian bishop.

Many persons in all ages have read this passage again and again, and have regarded it as a most righteous law.

Moses did not establish slavery; nor did he originate the remarkable prophecy respecting slavery as a curse on the race of Ham. Moses dealt with slavery as an existing system, the abolition of which was beyond his control. Any thing approaching to the slave trade, the laws delivered by Moses punished with death; the penalty which attached to the crime of man-stealing was, "He that stealeth a man shall surely be put to death."

But here was a whole race of slaves; not a few men stolen from their homes and compelled to serve, but a whole race under the mysterious ban of servitude, which no earthly power could have, or ever has, removed. Moses, then, had only to lay down laws for the proper treatment of the slave; and to lay them down not merely for the slave, but also with regard to the position of the master, to lay down just laws; for the slave was the property of his master—in fact "his money." Slavery is a terrible curse; but the slave was then, and is now, in slave countries, the property of his master. But, under the Jewish law, the master had not the power of life and death.

Horace speaks of one who would crucify his slave for merely gobbling up, when removing the remains of the supper, the half-eaten fishes and the sauce; and he says, that such a man would be counted more insane than the special type of a madman whom he selects. This is where Horace pleads that punishment should always be dealt out in proportion to the nature of the crime. And this, which Horace learned from the light of nature—from those eternal and immutable laws which the Creator has written as with a sunbeam—was precisely what Moses here laid down.

We have various terms for the taking away of life, "wilful murder," "manslaughter," "justifiable homicide," "accidental death." What would be thought of our sense of justice, if we were to visit with life for life the person whose act might come under the last two cases—make no difference between wilful murder and justifiable homicide or accidental death—but hang indiscriminately under all those circumstances?

This rash mode of punishment was all that Moses

forbad. And he laid down principles of justice which were to rule the decisions of the judges; and if a man beat a slave, and the slave did not die under his hand, but perhaps died some time afterwards, it was not a case of wilful murder—where blood would be required for blood; as the presumption would be that the master would not wilfully kill his slave, seeing that the slave was his property—" his money."

We do not write merely to answer Bishop Colenso; and, therefore, we have in this, as in other instances, enlarged on the subject of his objections, because they furnish occasion for useful information; and, chiefly, to show specimens of the wretched system of arguing by which Bishop Colenso endeavours to undermine and destroy the credibility of the Holy Scriptures.

But, some may exclaim, slavery is a cursed system, and surely you would not plead for its existence. Nothing can be farther from our mind, or our desire. But we say to the most bitter and malignant hater of the Bible,—who, like Satan in his address to the Sun, would desire it to shine out " that I may tell thee how I hate thy beams;"—we would say to such a man,—The Bible did not invent or establish slavery: and, unless you contend for the absurdity that the world was created and is governed by chance, you must look upon slavery as a most mysterious and painful Providential infliction on the human race.

And, after all, what is the worst form of slavery, and its most debased and debasing effects, when compared with the horrors and effects of slavery under the cursed domination of vice — a slavery not confined to the doomed race of Ham, but a slavery spread over all nations, and the tyrant of every age, and clime, and people? This slavery robs a man of all property in himself, breaks and casts to the wind every social tie, brings its victims down from the image of God below the level of the brute creation, and converts earth into a den of murderers—into a very hell.

And the worst feature in this slavery is, that, whereas the poor slave of the race of Ham receives daily food, and like

> "God's image disinherited of day,
> Here, plunged in mines, forgets a sun was made;"

he may, under some circumstances, forget his chain; or, even unconscious of its existence, may regard his home as the "happiest spot below."

> "The naked negro, panting at the line,
> Boasts of his golden sands and palmy wine,
> Basks in the glare, or stems the tepid wave,
> And thanks his Gods for all the good they gave."

There is some truth beneath those simple and beautiful lines. Still, while writing thus, we fully adopt the sentiments in the well-known words of another writer, "Disguise thyself as thou wilt, still, slavery, thou art a bitter draught; and though thousands have, in all ages, been made to drink of thee, thou art not the less bitter on that account." However, what we have said holds good; but the poor slave of vice does not receive any wages in return for the hard bondage with which he is made to serve. "Now therefore, what have I here, saith Jehovah, that My people is taken away for nought? They that rule over them make them to howl, saith the Lord; and My name continually every day is blasphemed."

Here, then, Bishop Colenso, we have something like a difficulty; a difficulty greater than Moses saying that the slave was his master's money; and a difficulty that rises far above your petty difficulties founded on your application of your plus and minus, your square feet and square yards, your measurement of the Court of Tabernacles, to find out how many human beings may be crowded into the same!

And must we learn from you, in the exercise of your functions as a Christian Bishop, to conclude, that the books of Nature, of Providence, and of Grace, in which these dreadful difficulties are recorded,—difficulties "written with a pen of iron, and point of a diamond,"—are mere compilations of fables and lies?

CHAPTER X.

Further consideration of objections—The Family of Judah—Way in which this point is viewed by others—The Bishop's mode of arguing—The Bishop not to be believed, unless he prove his commission to deliver a new Revelation—The size of the Tabernacle—The Bishop's ludicrous assumptions and arguments—His *petitio principii* here as in all his writing—Moses never meant any thing so absurd as that with which Bishop Colenso charges him—The Bishop's wish father to his thought in this attack on Moses—Moses and Joshua reading in the hearing of all the people—The Bishop's laughable view of this—Common-sense meaning—Arguing on the ludicrous view of the Bishop would overthrow the whole Revelation of God—The speaking-trumpet—The trumpet of Alexander the Great—The littleness of such objections—The extent of the Camp—The Bishop's originality in this objection—Absurdity of his argument—Will afford much laughter to infidels.

FAMILY OF JUDAH.

IN treating this question in such a way as to involve the sacred writers in contradiction to themselves, the Bishop's point is, that Hezron and Hamul, sons of Pharez, "*were born in the land of Canaan.*" This, the Bishop says, "*appears to me certain, that the writer here means to say so much.*" The inspired writer says, that threescore and ten persons, the family of

Jacob, went down into Egypt. And in Genesis we read, threescore and six persons, besides Jacob's sons' wives. And the sons of Joseph, with Jacob and Joseph, would make up the threescore and ten of the family, then settlers in Egypt.

When we read of the family of Jacob that went down into Egypt and settled there with their father, we think of the promise of God to Abraham, of which that little band was the depositary; that promise of Him "who keepeth His covenant for ever," and on which countless millions have in all ages suspended their hopes—even in the land of captivity and affliction; and without hope in which the afflictions of time would drive men mad, by sending them forth as wanderers upon earth, with a burden as heavy and insupportable as his who cried out, "My punishment is greater than I can bear." Such is our view. But Bishop Colenso would teach us very different theology!

The Bishop finds only proof of the falsehood of the history in the reference to this family; and really we must confess that we cannot see the point on which the Bishop dwells with as much earnestness as if he were working out a plan for the salvation of the human race.

He seems to puzzle himself, and seek to perplex others, as to the precise meaning of the terms, "went down with Jacob into Egypt," and as to the way in which the number threescore and ten is made up; and also as to whether two of the sons of Pharez were born in the land of Canaan. And because he cannot see all this in the light in which he decides that it should be, and which he so desires, he denounces the whole history as fable.

And suppose that we were to enter on such wretched cavils, and go on the presumption that we know all this better than the great man who wrote the facts, and who was just as careful as, and much more competent to guard against any contradictions to himself than, Bishop Colenso; on what grounds —except that he does not, and cannot see all this as plainly as Moses did who wrote the statement, —on what grounds does the Bishop found his reasoning?

"It appears to me to be certain that the writer here means," &c. . . . . "I assume, then, that it is absolutely undeniable that the narrative of the exodus distinctly involves the statement," &c. Then he gives the age which he says Judah was when he went down with his father Jacob. Then the sum is worked out by reference to the age of Joseph, and to the difference between his age and the age of Judah when he was born, and other points of such littleness.

Really, apart from any other consideration than the mere folly and want of any result, as appears to us, we must say, that we cannot make any thing of all this expenditure of wisdom and ingenuity on the part of the Bishop. He is not, it is true, bound to find brains for his reader; but we have looked again and again at his words, and we cannot find out the least point to prove that Moses could not—if we had an opportunity of conversing with him—reconcile any seeming difficulty, arising only from the Bishop's view of the phrase, "going down into Egypt," and "out of his loins."

It is a pitiable sight to see any man, much more a Christian Bishop, make such an exhibition of himself, by trying, on such contemptible grounds, to unsettle the faith of men by denying and insulting the Revelation of the Creator to the lost race of Adam; for, until the Bishop can produce a revelation, and exhibit his credentials for the truth of the same, he must excuse us if we refuse to believe one word of his learned work.

Did the Bishop, when he descended to such petty play on words, ever reflect on the woe denounced against those " who make a man an offender for a word?" or did he ever read the beautiful words of Hooker, where he expresses his gratitude, that in reference to God our Judge we have to do, not with a captious sophister who only seeks to find out faults, but with a gracious and merciful Being who is ever anxious to make the best of what, from regard for Him, we endeavour to perform?

We do not thus write as if the sacred writers, whom the Bishop seeks to involve in contradictions to themselves, required any consideration or apology. We do not fear for them. They need not any defence.

—— " Non tali auxilio
Nec defensoribus istis—tempus eget."

But we do feel for Bishop Colenso, as we should for any man who could by such a book so degrade that spark of Deity—the reason which God, for very different ends, has bestowed on the human race.

THE SIZE OF THE COURT OF THE TABERNACLE COMPARED WITH THE NUMBER OF THE CONGREGATION.

The Bishop commences this proof of the Pentateuch being a fable, with the words—" And Jehovah spake unto Moses, saying, ... Gather thou all the congregation together unto the door of the tabernacle of the congregation. And Moses did as Jehovah commanded him. And the assembly was gathered unto the door of the tabernacle of the congregation."

To build on these words an argument to prove that Moses wrote fables and lies, Bishop Colenso, in his usual way of reasoning, begins by assuming that all men, women, women on the point of bringing forth, and children—even infants in the arms—must have been crowded into the space which he, on his principles of arithmetic, propounds. He lays great stress on "*adults in the prime of life.*" Sick, bed-ridden, and all must have been packed into the small space which the Bishop calculates was the exact size of the court of the tabernacle. Or else, when Moses wrote the above verse, he wrote a fable and a lie; and, therefore, his history is fable and falsehood. And all the other sacred writers, and even the Redeemer Himself, were guilty of collusion with Moses in seeking to impose fables and lies on the race of man.

"First," writes the Bishop, " it appears to be certain, that by the expressions used so often, here and elsewhere,—' the assembly,' ' the whole assembly,' ' all the congregation,' — is meant the whole body of the people;—at all events, *the adult males in the prime of life.*" (These important italics are the Bishop's). And he would show that all the adult males in the prime of life of a large nation could not have been packed into a small courtyard; and that, therefore, Moses was a liar, as well as a fool;—a liar, to say any such thing; and a fool, to imagine that not merely the Bishop, but that any man in his senses, could believe such " a fact."

The Bishop then rises in his critical powers as if he had a growing consciousness of his strength; and, after some quotations to prove his first assumption, he, waxing bolder, says, "It might reasonably be inferred," that is, from some of *his* proofs of *his* assumption, or, if we soar into the region of science, his *petitio principii*, or, in plain language for the English reader, his begging of the question,—" It might," he says, " be inferred," that "the women also, and *children* (the italics here, too, are the Bishop's), would be included in the whole congregation," who were to be packed and squeezed into the courtyard. Poor women, and poor children! your sufferings must have been great indeed, and which you could not have borne as well as "*the adult males in the prime of life;*" and, indeed, the "adult males" themselves must have perished by multitudes, if Moses sought to pack them into such a small space.

On the Bishop's testimony, all this packing, squeezing, and crying of children, and groaning of adults, must have taken place; for, in another place, to prove the impossibility of the voice of Moses, or of Joshua, reaching to the utmost extent of the people, the Bishop suggests, in the spirit of a true philosopher, that the crying of the infants must have hindered such a result! But the misfortune for the Bishop's onslaught on the wisdom and Word of God—for we are not to be overawed into the belief of his infidelity by such arguments as he and his school produce, and therefore we continue to assume that Moses wrote the truth of God;—but, we say, the misfortune for the Bishop's argument is, that Moses never wrote or even imagined any such thing.

But, the Bishop would say—" does he not say, 'gather thou all the congregation together unto the door of the tabernacle?' And I say, that means the whole nation, men, adults, males in the prime of life, elders, heads of people, women and children, sick and afflicted included; and therefore they must have been all, not only in the court, but at the door. But as this could not be the case, the whole history is a fable, and Moses wrote to deceive mankind!"

Well, certainly, Moses does say, "Gather thou all the congregation together unto the door of the tabernacle of the congregation;" but as to the Bishop's second position, that this meant the packing of the whole nation, all ranks, all classes, and all ages, sick as well as those in health, into a courtyard, we require some little better proof that Moses was a fool or a liar, and we think that he understood what he wrote much better than does Bishop Colenso in his "First it appears to be certain that by the expressions so used is meant," &c. &c.; and "From some of the above passages indeed it might be reasonably inferred," &c. &c.

We do not want "It appears to be certain," or "It might be reasonably inferred:" we want something far more positive as the premises from which to draw such a conclusion as that the writings of Moses are fables and lies—lies, as we have repeatedly urged, of the deepest dye, because lies spoken in the name and as the very words of the Almighty.

The Bishop then applies his knowledge of arithmetic, and having proved the exact size of the court, the square feet and yards, &c., concludes with his "*must*"—must, according to the words of Moses, have been squeezed into the small space so learnedly calculated by Bishop Colenso. Was ever more "learned nonsense" written by any man? Surely the mind that could stoop to such wretched cavilling must have been first poisoned by infidelity, and then have sought to find every petty excuse to blot out the Book of truth and life. The wish to involve Moses in such ridiculous contradictions and folly must, indeed, have been "father to the thought" of the Bishop of Natal.

MOSES AND JOSHUA ADDRESSING ALL THE PEOPLE.

Another of the objections of the Bishop of Natal to the truth of the Holy Scriptures is, "the reading of the law in the hearing of all the people."

Here, then, was some room for calculation. So far this objection differs from that founded on the "dumb ass speaking with man's voice." But it must be an exercise of the mind, in what degree it is not our business to inquire, to find out the exact space within which a man can be confined, and then to multiply that space by some other quantity would give the result as to the space which the whole people filled; and then would arise another question to be solved—the exact distance to which the air would convey sound, and make the human voice to be heard.

There may be very great learning concealed beneath all this, but we must confess that we cannot discover the hidden store. And, so far as we can call to mind, we do not think that Paine or other infidels hit upon this grand idea by which the truth of Revelation is overthrown by the Christian Bishop of Natal!

We do not mean to take up our time or that of our readers by an explanation of such a simple phrase, which most certainly did not call for such a waste of time and learning. We all know the meaning: that public acts of all kingdoms are said to be done before, and in the hearing of the nations. This phraseology prevails in reference to courts of justice, though confined by walls within a very small space, and a man tried within those walls is tried in the face of England, and the court is open to all England, and all is done before all England as well as in the sight of the sun.

When Solomon dedicated the temple, it is said, "The king turned his face and blessed the whole congregation, and all the congregation of Israel stood;" and again, "And he stood before the altar of the Lord in the presence of all the congregation of Israel."

And when John the Baptist came to preach the way of the Lord, it is said, "Then went out to him Jerusalem, and all Judea, and all the region round about

Jordan, and were baptized of him in Jordan confessing their sins."

Now we suppose it unnecessary to say that some did not hear the blessing of Solomon; that *all* did not see him when he stood in the presence of all the congregation of Israel; that some men, women, and children, though it was open to them to come, were not there at all, and that some were detained by sickness or other casualties from forming part of the congregation on that day. And let us in like manner conclude as to Jerusalem and all Judea going out to be baptized of John in the river Jordan. Must we then, on the principle laid down by Bishop Colenso, conclude that the whole history of these events, including the very existence of Solomon and John the Baptist, is all mere fable and falsehood?

Such new principles of reasoning would not deserve serious notice, but that they treat of sacred subjects, and show the extent to which men may go when they once break loose from the pastures where true wisdom is to be found, and wander over the barren mountains of pride and vanity. Can, we ask, as in former instances, can Bishop Colenso imagine, that, if there were any difficulty as to this mode of speech, it escaped the inspired writers who make the statement; or that it escaped all the inspired writers who followed until the canon of Scripture was complete, and all of whom believed in the book which on such most contemptible littlenesses Bishop Colenso insults and seeks to overthrow?

We will not here suppose that Moses or Joshua employed agents to convey to the more distant the words which they read, and on the principle of "quod facit per alium facit per se," might have been said to have done that which they did by others. Nor need we, in order to uphold the truth of the Holy Scriptures against such childish attacks, suggest, for we have as much right to suggest as the Bishop has to assume, and his work is little else than the assumption that all his views are "the truth," which must in the end prevail to overthrow the whole Bible — we need not then suggest that perhaps Joshua used a speaking-trumpet. The Bishop, were we to seriously thus argue, might reply, "No! that was not possible, for the speaking-trumpet was not invented," and therefore the truth of the Bishop, founded on this amazingly little objection, must stand against all writers, inspired or uninspired.

But we might rejoin that, though the invention of the speaking-trumpet be attributed to Sir Samuel Morland, yet it was known and used in the Swiss mountains to summon to public worship people at a distance of from two to five Italian miles. And what shall we say of the extraordinary trumpet of Alexander the Great; a copy of which, from the print at Rome in the Vatican, we have in Derham's Boyle Lectures, by which Alexander could send his orders to the distance of one hundred stadia?

Suppose, then, that Joshua had known and used such, then we suppose that in this way he might have conveyed his words to the ears of all the people in the most literal sense of the term, and then this one very formidable arrow of Bishop Colenso against the truth of Holy Scripture might have been extracted from his so plentifully supplied quiver, his *gravida sagittis Pharetra*. But all this is mere folly and idle waste of time, and only to be surpassed by the folly which deserves not sympathy, but the most severe reproof, which could from such premises draw the conclusion that inspired writings are mere fables and lies.

THE EXTENT OF THE CAMP, &c.

This is in truth the Bishop's own. In this chapter he is original. His difficulty here is, that the priest himself must have carried all the ashes and all the filth a distance of three-quarters of a mile, on one supposition,—so wonderfully accurate is the Bishop in these wise and most learned investigations—and upwards of six miles, according to another of his minute and yet great calculations; and that all the people, including "aged and infirm, women in childbirth, sick persons, and young children," must, according to what Moses wrote, have gone on every occasion all those so learnedly calculated distances for "the common necessities of nature!" and because they could not have done this—then here is a most unanswerable proof that the Pentateuch is pure fable and lie!

We could say something more on this grand part of the Bishop's argument, but we pass it by as it best deserves, and only remark, that we have not learned philosophy to such an extent as to make not merely the truth of the Pentateuch, or even of Cæsar's Commentaries, or the book of the father of history, Herodotus, depend on the way which the armies of Cæsar, or the wonderful army of Xerxes, found to cleanse their camps; whether that work was done by the generals, and how the people, men, women, children, "aged and infirm, women in childbirth, sick persons, and young children," found to attend day by day to "the common necessities of nature."

Oh, Bishop Colenso! "O tempora! O mores!" By this one proof at least of Moses having written fable and falsehood you have immortalized yourself; and, in ages to come, when your name and book shall have been forgotten, infidels, such as those whom you now cause to rejoice over Moses and the other inspired " witnesses" whom you have slain, as you and they, —but yet not Satan, for he knows better,—suppose, when they spend their nights in reviling " Moses and the Prophets," and Apostles, will convulse the midnight assembly with laughter, when they discuss this most original and yet not most refined argument of some African bishop (not Cyprian or St. Augustine) of former days, whose name and work the witty infidel does not just then remember.

CHAPTER XI.

Increase of the posterity of Abraham—The consequence of a special promise and blessing of Providence—Referred to repeatedly and openly on many occasions by Moses and the other Sacred Writers—By those writers, the increase so viewed—Bishop Colenso would bind down the Creator by his poor standard—Laplace and Napoleon—The Book of Nature's testimony—Great difference in the amount of increase—The Parable of the Sower—Pliny's account of fertility in some soil—The variations of Nature too uncertain for such conclusions as Bishop Colenso would draw—Instances of wonderful increase in some families—The testimony of a Christian Philosopher to the wisdom and power of God, in reference to the population of the earth.

As Bishop Colenso refers, in several chapters of his objections against the Holy Scriptures, to the extraordinary increase of the descendants of Abraham, as furnishing an argument for the overthrow of Moses and the writings which bear his name, we propose now to examine the subject in such way as to not merely test the soundness of the Bishop's mode of arguing, but at the same time to bring forward matter which may be instructive and profitable to the lay portion of our readers, who may not have given much attention to the subjects now under discussion.

The seed of Abraham inherited the promise, that they should be as the stars of heaven for multitude, and as the sand of the sea innumerable; and this promise Moses has recorded as the promise of God to the Father of the Faithful; and Moses further writes, that the seed of Abraham did multiply, even in the land of their hard bondage, like the palm growing under pressure. Moses also appealed to the people on this very head, as showing the faithfulness of God in keeping the promise to Abraham—" so shall thy seed be." Also Gen. xiii., "And I will make thy seed as the dust of the earth," &c.

When Balak sent for Balaam to curse the seed of Abraham, he thus described them: "Behold, there is a people come out from Egypt: behold, they cover the face of the earth." And when Balaam was overruled in his intention to curse them, he said, "Who can count the dust of Jacob, and the number of the fourth part of Israel?" And when he took leave of the children of Israel, Moses said, "The Lord your God hath multiplied you; and, behold, ye are this day as the stars of heaven for multitude." And again, "Thy fathers went down into Egypt with threescore and ten persons, and now the Lord thy God hath made thee as the stars of heaven for multitude."

Such is the account given by Moses of the promise of God, and of its fulfilment to the seed of Abraham: and Moses ascribes this fulfilment of the promise to the exercise of God's special Providence; for he does not speak of this as the usual acting of nature. He attributes the increase to the promises and to the special exercise of the Providence of God, exercised in bringing about, not any thing contrary to nature, but yet a result contrary to the history and experience of other nations.

Now, in all this Moses wrote mere fable and falsehood in the name of God;—for Bishop Colenso has applied to this question his *plus* and *minus*, and his calculations from blue-books; and he has fixed so many persons born, and so many marriages, and so many children as the fruit of each marriage, and so many as the increase of mankind in a generation; and, therefore, the Almighty must be bound down by the statistics of Bishop Colenso! And Moses must have been a fool, and worse, for having published such a fable; and for having sought to impose on the credulity of mankind by such falsehoods!

Regard for our own time, and for that of our readers, and for mere common sense, will not allow us to trouble ourselves about these statistics, which Bishop Colenso, by his knowledge of arithmetic, and his application of figures, fixes as the standard which he will allow. We deal with the point very differently; and only to show how little competent the Bishop is to lay down his standard as the unerring law of nature, and to reason from such standard against the wisdom and veracity of Moses, who wrote the account; and against the promise of God, to which the increase of the nation was and is to be attributed.

This attempt of Bishop Colenso to hedge Moses in, and convict him of fable and falsehood by the Bishop's lines and angles—his *plus* and *minus*—forces on our mind the history of Napoleon and Laplace. But we must first beg of our readers not to imagine for a moment that we make light of lines and angles, *plus* and *minus*, as terms of a great science, and as modes of reasoning. No such thing. There is not any difference between reasoning by such signs and figures, and reasoning by words, as so many lines and angles, and signs of the thing signified. We do not find any fault with such in themselves; but we do find fault with the way in which they are by some minds applied to such purposes as finding out puzzles, just as we should find fault with some blundering carpenter or mechanic for the stupid and profitless use which he would make of implements in his hands, implements in themselves capable of producing grand results.

Napoleon, dazzled, in common with others, by the splendour of the fame which Laplace acquired by his mathematics, thought that the employment of such a man in his cabinet would greatly strengthen his own rule as Consul, and be no small service to the State. Well, Laplace was appointed, but he made a sorry minister; so that he had to be put aside almost as soon as he was appointed. Whenever Napoleon had any great question before him, there was even the great Laplace, with his lines and angles, his *plus* and *minus*, all, as we have said, good in themselves, but out of place and misapplied, measuring every question by his minute calculations; seeking only objections and difficulties, and impeding all business. So Napoleon, having greatness not to be thus confined, had to get rid of the mathematician as the only hope of having any important work done. An excuse might be pleaded for Laplace, one, too, which would apply to Bishop Colenso. The fault was not in mathematics.

But, to return to the point,—the increase of the people. Let us learn from nature, which is always true to itself, and in whose book we find what the Almighty does, and does before the eyes of the greatest infidel. The wheat is cast into the ground; the produce must depend on the soil, and on the rain and sunshine of heaven: for, when man has done his part in preparing the soil, and sowing the seed, he can do no more. He may follow any other occupation, or he may give himself up to idleness and ease. For, if he were to watch and work, and work and watch, all day and night, he cannot go beyond the limit prescribed by God. The Creator then takes the matter into His own hands. But, though all increase thus depends on the care of Him who does not slumber nor sleep,—who giveth the former and the latter rain in its season,—and who has thus challenged the pretensions of idols to make the seed to grow: " Are there any among the vanities of the Gentiles that can cause rain, or can the earth give showers?" yet, notwithstanding that the produce from the seed sown has the benefit of such care, how very unequal the return from that seed sown in the earth, the inequality depending on a variety of circumstances almost altogether beyond the control of man!

Thus, for instance, when the Lord Jesus delivers the parable of the sower, He shows the difference to be from the soil in which the seed is sown; and that difference is very great, ranging from one hundred down to thirtyfold. He does not assume a higher standard than one hundredfold.

But Pliny gives instances of the fertility of some countries, where the soil produced very much more than the hundredfold mentioned in this parable. Speaking of wheat, which grows in every clime, from those regions which are " the courtiers of the sun, and wait upon him in his chambers of the east," to those countries " where Phœbus' fire scarce thaws the icicles," he writes, " which fertility nature hath conferred upon it, because it feeds man with it; one bushel, if sown in a fit and proper soil, such as is Byzachium, a field in Africa, yielding one hundred and fifty of annual increase. Augustus' procurator sent him from that place four hundred, within a few blades, springing from the same grain; and to Nero were sent thence three hundred and sixty." "If Pliny, a heathen, could make this fertility of wheat argumentative of the bounty of God to man, making such plentiful provision for him of that which is most pleasant to taste and wholesome nourishment, surely it ought not to be passed over by us Christians without notice-taking and thanksgiving."

But, if we adopt the Bishop of Natal's principle of *reasoning*, instead of admiring the wonderful goodness of our Creator to earth and its ungrateful inhabitants, we should at once place our blessed Lord and Pliny in direct opposition to each other, and make each accuse the other of sending forth a fabulous account, and thus condemn all their other sayings or writings. For instance, on his method of treating the question, the Bishop might urge that the whole account given by Pliny of such increase was quite contrary to a fact which he had learned by experiments made in some little garden, and by something that he had learned from a great man for statistics; and that it was impossible that a single grain of wheat could have yielded any thing like the percentage alleged; and that, therefore, the whole account must be a mere fable, and the other parts of Pliny's work no better; and that, moreover, when the highest authority gave the increase of wheat when sown in good soil, He stated one hundredfold as the largest return.

On the other hand, a believer in Pliny might, in a similar way, turn round and assert the Gospel statement to be a mere fable, because it stated one hundredfold as the maximum increase; whereas he knew a fact which proved that in Africa wheat produced many times more than the return stated in the Gospel.

But why do we thus notice this subject? Not to prove the wisdom and truth of Moses in reply to Bishop Colenso, but to show the nature of those premises from which Bishop Colenso draws the conclusion that Moses was an inventor of fables and falsehoods, and a wilful deceiver of mankind.

The old well-known line contains much truth:

"Naturam furcâ expellas, tamen usque recurret."

To seek then to force nature within our contracted standard, to say of her operations, they must be according to this or that rule, to Bishop Colenso's standard of *plus* and *minus*, and blue-books, is the very height of absurdity and presumption. Shakespeare well said, "An habitation giddy and unsure hath he that buildeth on the vulgar heart."

No better definition of the fickleness of man was ever propounded, if we except the " Hosannah to the son of David, blessed is he that cometh in the name of the Lord," from the very same multitude that afterwards shouted, "Crucify Him, crucify Him."

And if this be true, as true it is, what are we to say to a mathematician who would ask us to build arguments on the shifting sands of the varieties and indeed freaks of nature? We might as well conclude that all men should be born without defect, because God made man so perfect in form as man has been made, and because we might say that it should be so, as that mankind should increase only in the way prescribed by the new lords of nature, the Bishop of Natal and his followers.

We have thus given some account of the variations

of nature in reference to the seed sown in the womb of mother earth. Let us now come back from the variations of nature, in reference to seed sown in the ground, to the history of our race.

We know, as well as Bishop Colenso, the usual calculations of so many births as the result of each marriage; but we shall not follow his mode of arguing from premises as absolutely certain, which are founded on the most uncertain of all things, the variations of nature. When Horace spoke of the St. Januarius imposition of his day, he did not deny the fact of wonderful things in nature, and of variations from its usual course. He contented himself with the idea, that if nature did exhibit those wonderful departures from its usual course, the matter was to be reconciled on the Epicurean system, that the gods spent a very indolent and jovial life, and did not concern themselves about such little things as the variations in the domain of nature,—

"—— Namque Deos didici securum agere ævum;
Nec, si quid miri faciat natura, Deos id
Tristes ex alto cœli demittere tecto."

Now, from some marriages an only child is the result. On the other hand, we ourselves know of three instances in which women had, two of them twenty-three, and, one of them, twenty-four children each; and, to pass from our own knowledge to days gone by, we will give a few facts.

We shall not dwell on the seventy sons of Ahab, or on such like instances derived from Eastern nations. We come to more modern times. "Babo, Earl of Abensperg, had thirty-two sons and eight daughters; and, being invited to hunt with the Emperor Henry II., and bring but few servants, brought only one servant and his thirty-two sons. To these many others might be added; but one of the most remarkable instances I have any where met with, is that of Mrs. Honeywood, mentioned by Hakewill, Camden, and other authors; but having now before me the names, with some remarks, which I received from a pious neighbouring descendant of the same Mrs. Honeywood, I shall give a more particular account than they.

"Mrs. Mary Honeywood was daughter, and one of the co-heiresses, of Robert Atwaters, Esq., of Lenham, in Kent. She was born in 1527, married in February 1543, at sixteen years of age, to her only husband Robert Honeywood, of Charing in Kent, Esq. She died in the ninety-third year of her age, in May, 1620. She had sixteen children of her own body, seven sons, and nine daughters; of which one had no issue. Three died young, and the youngest was slain at Newport battle, June 20, 1600. Her grandchildren, in the second generation, were 114; in the third, 228; and nine in the fourth generation (900!). So that she could say the same that the distich doth, made of one of the Dalburg's family of Basil:—

'Mater ait Natæ, dic Natæ, filia Natam,
Ut moneat, Natæ, plangere Filiolam.'

' Rise up, Daughter, and go to thy Daughter,
For her Daughter's Daughter hath a Daughter.'"

We conclude these remarks with a passage from a Christian philosopher, which will well repay the reader for its perusal.

"The whole surface of our globe can afford room

and support only to such a number of all sorts of creatures; and if by their doubling, trebling, or any other multiplication of their kind, they should increase to double or treble that number, they must starve, or devour one another. The keeping, therefore, the balance even, is manifestly a work of the Divine wisdom and Providence. To which end the great Author of life hath determined the life of all creatures to such a length, and their increase to such a number, proportional to their use in the world.

"The life of some creatures is long, and their increase but small, and by that means they do not overstock the world. And the same benefit is effected where the increase is great, by the brevity of such creatures' lives, by their great use and the frequent occasions there are of them for food to man, or other animals. It is a very remarkable act of the Divine Providence that useful creatures are produced in great plenty, and others in less. The prodigious and frequent increase of insects, both in and out of the waters, may exemplify the one; and 'tis observable in the other that creatures less useful, or by their voracity pernicious, have commonly fewer young, or do seldomer bring forth enough, and then only enough, to keep up the species, but not to overcharge the world.

"Thus the balance of the animal world is, throughout all ages, kept even; and by a curious harmony, and just proportion between the increase of all animals, and the length of their lives, the world is through all ages well, but not over-stored: 'one generation passeth away, and another generation cometh;' so equally in its room to balance the stock of the terraqueous globe in all ages and places, and among all creatures, that it is an actual demonstration of our Saviour's assertion, Matt. x. 2. 9, that the most inconsiderable common creature, 'even a sparrow (two of which are sold for a farthing), doth not fall on the ground without our heavenly Father.'

"This Providence of God is remarkable in every species of living creatures: but that especial management of the recruits and decays of mankind, so equally all the world over, deserves our especial observation. In the beginning of the world, and so after Noah's flood, the longevity of men, as it was of absolute necessity to the more speedy peopling of the new world, so is a special instance of the Divine Providence in this matter. And the same Providence appears in the following ages, when the world was pretty well peopled, in reducing the common age of man then to one hundred and twenty years (Gen. vi. 3), in proportion to the occasions of the world at that time.

"And, lastly, when the world was fully peopled, after the flood (as it was in the age of Moses, and so down to our present time), the lessening the common age of man to seventy or eighty years (the age mentioned by Moses, Ps. xc. 10),—this, I say, is manifestly an appointment of the same Infinite LORD that ruleth the world. For by this means, the peopled world is kept at a convenient stay, neither too full nor too empty.

"For, if men (the generality of them, I mean) were to live now to Methuselah's age of nine hundred and sixty-nine years, or only to Abraham's, long after the flood, of one hundred and seventy-five years, the world would be too much overrun; or, if the age of man was limited to that of diverse other animals, to ten, twenty, or thirty years only, the decays then of mankind would be too fast. But at the middle rate mentioned, the balance is nearly even, and life and death keeps an equal pace: which equality is so great and harmonious, and so manifest an instance of the Divine management, that I shall spend some remarks upon it.

"It appears from our best accounts of these matters, that, in our European parts, and I believe the same is throughout the world,—that, I say, there is a certain rate and proportion in the propagation of mankind. Such a number marry; so many are born; such a number die; in proportion to the number of persons in every nation, county, or parish. And as to births, two things are very considerable: one is, the proportion of males and females not in a wide proportion; not an uncertain, accidental number at all adventures, but nearly equal. Another thing is, that a few more are born than appear to die in any certain place; which is an admirable provision for the extraordinary emergencies and occasions of the world;—to supply unhealthful places, where death outruns life; to make up the ravages of great plagues and diseases, and the depredations of war and the seas; and to afford a sufficient number for colonies in the unpeopled parts of the earth.

"Or, on the other hand, we may say that sometimes those extraordinary expences of mankind may be not only a just punishment of the sins of men, but also a wise means to keep the balance of mankind even, as one would be ready to conclude, by considering the Asiatic, and other the more fertile countries, where prodigious multitudes are yearly swept away with great plagues, and sometimes war, and yet those countries are so far from being wasted, that they remain full of people.

"And now, upon the whole matter, what is all this but admirable and plain management? What can the maintaining, throughout all ages and places, these proportions of mankind, and all other creatures, this harmony in the generations of men, be, but the work of One that ruleth the world? Is it possible that every species of animals should so evenly be preserved, proportionate to the occasions of the world; that they should be so well balanced in all ages and places, without the help of Almighty Wisdom and Power? How it is possible, by the bare rules, and blind acts of Nature, that there should be any tolerable proportions; for instance, between males and females, either of mankind or any other creature, especially such as are of a fierce, not of a domestic nature, and consequently out of the command and management of man?

"How could life and death keep such an even pace through all the animal world, if we should take it for granted, that, according to the Scripture history, the world had a beginning (as who can deny it? or, if we should suppose the destruction thereof by Noah's flood, how is it possible after the world was replenished?) that in a certain number of years, by the greater increases and doublings of each species of animals, that, I say, this rate of doubling should cease; or, that it should be compensated by some other means; that the world should be as well, or better stocked, than now it is, in 1656 years (the time between the creation and the flood)? This, we will suppose, may be done by the natural method of each species doubling or increase. But in double that number of years, or at this distance from the flood, of 4000 years, that the world should not be overstocked, can never be made out, without allowing an Infinite Providence.

"I conclude, then, this observation with the Psalmist's words (Ps. civ. 29, 30), 'Thou hidest Thy face, all creatures are troubled; Thou takest away their breath, they die, and return to their dust. Thou sendest forth

Thy Spirit, they are created; and Thou renewest the face of the earth[1].'"

We leave Bishop Colenso to work out this problem, and to explain to any one gifted with the least portion of common sense, how he can pretend to lay down as " the truth," premises based on such variations and inconstancies of Nature ; and then to draw from such premises a conclusion by which he gives the lie direct to such a writer as Moses;—and by which he thinks, poor man! to shake the foundation of Faith, and overthrow the Revelation of God to Man.

CHAPTER XII.

Dwelling in Tents—Bishop Colenso's impossibilities—His childish suppositions as to carriage of such by men or oxen—Nadir Shah and the sacking of Delhi—Great armies not at any loss to carry their baggage—The absurdity of Bishop Colenso in seeking to destroy the veracity of Holy Writ by such arguments—The Israelites armed—The Bishop's absurd notions on this head—The Bishop's cavilling on this would have been despised by infidels of past ages—The Passover—The Bishop's ludicrous difficulties on this question—The Passover, notwithstanding the Bishop's notions, was established and observed in all ages—The march out of Egypt referred to by the Sacred Writers—The Bishop's laughable proof of the impossibility of this march—His fright, and sudden flight—Not a fit man for the Church militant in Natal—Contrast with Nehemiah—Sheep and Cattle in the Desert—The Bishop's strange notion as to the neglect of the cattle—Folly of such reasoning—God's care of all His creatures—Cicero and Seneca on this—The valuable remarks of Derham on this subject—The Bishop would tie down the hand of the Almighty to his little rules.

THE ISRAELITES DWELLING IN TENTS.

IF ever the Sacred Writers put forth an absurdity and falsehood, it is the statement that the Israelites dwelt

[1] Derham's Boyle Lectures.

in tents. Bring what meaning you will, reader, out of the word "tents," yet, so far as the Israelites were concerned, the statement of Moses is pure falsehood. Robinson Crusoe might, even without the help of his man Friday, have built some kind of hut; and, thrown upon necessity "the mother of invention," the Bishop of Natal might, without the help of his Zulu, have constructed some kind of tent, tabernacle, booth—or any name you please,—to shelter him from the sun by day, and from the cold by night.

But so far as the poor Israelites were concerned, this was impossible. The gifts of reason, and the rich abundance of Nature, in every age and in every clime, to supply the wants of the creatures of God, were all bestowed in vain on the people of Israel.

And though the Israelites were commanded, as the Bishop allows, to take "boughs of goodly trees, branches of palm-trees, and boughs of thick trees, and willows of the brooks,"—yet none of these were to be considered as "tents." Indeed, it is—on Bishop Colenso's mode of arguing—most probable that all this about "goodly trees, branches of palm-trees, willows of the brooks" was mere fiction; for we have not any authority for it except that of the deceiver who wrote the Pentateuch, and who—according to a Christian Bishop—was only a forger of lies!

But suppose that this part of the Pentateuch were true, yet it is quite evident (to Bishop Colenso) that the matter of the "tents," mentioned in the same part of the work, was pure falsehood. How could the people have had tents? Take, we repeat, any meaning you please, reader, for the term. And, if they had them, how could they have carried such "cumbrous articles?" especially when they had to take their dough before it was leavened—"their kneading-troughs being bound up in their clothes upon their shoulders?"

G

There, sacred writers, is your death-blow! and there, reader, is a problem, which, if you can solve, you will throw the fame of Newton himself into the shade. But you must solve it on its own merits. How could the people carry such "cumbrous articles" as "*tents*," (the italics are the Bishop's,) with kneading-troughs, and all the other cumbrous articles which every man carried on his shoulders?

Now, reader, it will not do to assume that the people at large may have been considered as having done what some of them, appointed for special purposes under a division of labour, did; as armies are said to carry their baggage, guns, and many much more cumbrous articles than some kind of shelter for their heads from the sun by day or the dew by night. Nor will it avail to assume that, as one kneading-trough would suffice for more than one person, the others, who were not burdened with the carriage of them, might help to carry those things—call them tents, or what you please —which would serve for a covering.

Nor need you assume that oxen might help to carry any of those "cumbrous articles;" for the Bishop has settled that point. "There were the *cattle* certainly, which might have been turned to some account." But here was the difficulty—" turned to some account," "*if they had been trained to act as pack-oxen.*" "Ay, there's the rub,"—"*if they had been trained.*" How were the Israelites to train them—even though the ox be by nature made to serve in such way, and to be most patient of toil?

But suppose that point settled:—How do you get over this? Where were the people to find oxen enough for such a purpose? Nadir Shah, without any difficulty, found to hand, we think, five thousand camels, and nearly three thousand horses and mules, to carry away the mere plunder of Delhi, to the value of one hundred and twenty millions sterling; and that in addition to the conveyance of all the baggage of an army that covered a space of twelve miles wide, and we forget how many miles deep. And even Xerxes found means for the carriage of all things necessary for an army which, with the camp followers, amounted to several millions of human beings, not to speak of the cattle.

But it will not do to cite any instances of the kind. For, in order to make the writer of the Pentateuch a wilful liar and deceiver, it is self-evident (to Bishop Colenso), and it must be accepted as a fact by all mankind, that the Israelites could not have found means to carry their tents, even if they had any to carry, which, as we have allowed, was, with respect to the Israelites, an utter impossibility, because the Bishop of Natal says that it was an utter impossibility!

And thus Bishop Colenso demolishes the Holy Scriptures; that Revelation on which men have suspended all their hopes, and with feelings very different from those which the Jews experienced when they hanged their harps on the willows by the proud waters of Babylon. But we have had enough of this wretched mode of writing, and we are weary of examining such poor, and, in a Bishop, most discreditable and dishonourable cavilling at the word of God.

THE ISRAELITES ARMED.

On this point it is not necessary to say more than that Moses knew much better than Bishop Colenso the meaning of the word which he used when he wrote, "And the children of Israel went up harnessed out of the land of Egypt." A variety of meanings has been given to this word "harnessed;" which is a matter of very little moment. It may interest some minds to endeavour to find out the precise meaning, which must be difficult at this time, so remote from the period in which the words were written. And such search may have proved, and may prove, even profitable to those who have occupied themselves in the investigation.

It is, however, a very different question when the uncertainty of its meaning is used by any man to charge the writer with falsehood.

But Bishop Colenso gives his view of the word as "the truth," and then charges Moses with writing fables and lies, because, according to the Bishop's criticism, it was quite impossible that the people of Israel should have gone up "harnessed," or "armed," as the Bishop writes, out of the land of Egypt.

So far as we remember, infidels of old, from the days of the apostate Julian to the present time, took a higher flight than this of the Bishop of Natal, and never sought to deny the revelation of God on such little and childish grounds. But they might have learned something, if they had had the benefit of the instruction of a Christian Bishop of our day!

THE PASSOVER.

It was utterly impossible that the establishment of the passover, as described in the Pentateuch, could have taken place. How could Moses have conveyed so quickly the orders, which he says that he received from God, to a population equal to, if not greater than, that of London? And, even if that had been possible, how could the people have found lambs enough to take a lamb for a household? These are serious questions—further specimens of Bishop Colenso's difficulties.

The passover would certainly have required a very large number of lambs; not a doubt of this. And where were the Israelites to have found such a supply?

We shall not weary the reader with calculations as to the number of years which the children of Israel spent in Egypt, in the land of Goshen assigned to them on their first settlement, because they were shepherds. Nor shall we waste our time with calculations as to the number of sheep and lambs, which in a few centuries those patriarchs, whose wealth consisted in cattle, possessed.

In answer to such ridiculous questions, which cannot but overthrow the Revelation of God, at least according to Bishop Colenso's opinion, we shall only say, that, notwithstanding all this, it is a fact—and a better fact, we think, than the "fact" of the Bishop of Natal—that Moses did establish the passover, that he did persuade millions of men to believe and act upon what he said and commanded; and men who, as they knew the whole circumstances, could have exposed the fable and gross imposture, if any, and who, in consequence of their belief in this imposture, submitted to much inconvenience and sacrifice of property.

And, moreover, it is a fact that this passover was observed in all generations down to the Christian era, and was most reverently kept by the Redeemer with His disciples; and is most solemnly observed to this day by the people of Israel with this difference only, but yet great difference, that they do not sacrifice the lamb for the household, because, out of respect for that deceiver, Moses, and for the portion of the inspired writings which they receive, they cannot offer sacrifice on every altar or in every place, but only at the place which the Lord their God should "choose to place His Name there."

That place was first the tabernacle, and, after the days of Solomon, the temple. And, until the destruction of the temple, they always sacrificed the lamb as the chief part of the passover. But when "the Lamb of God, that taketh away the sin of the world," was to come, and "Christ our Passover" to be "sacrificed for us;" then, as Daniel foretold, the daily sacrifice and all sacrifice was to cease. Thus the children of Israel labour under an impossibility; and, though they keep the week of the passover, yet they cannot sacrifice. But they do observe the passover in accordance with this very appointment by Moses.

And yet, according to Bishop Colenso, the whole matter was an impossibility, and the statement of its institution only proves that Moses was a very wicked man for publishing any command of God for such an imposture; and that the book of Moses is fable and falsehood; and that Christianity is also an imposition on the human race; and its Founder one who gave sanction to such an act of impiety and falsehood as that of which Moses was guilty, in pretending to have been commissioned by Almighty God to establish an ordinance, which Bishop Colenso proves to have been an impossibility and a lie!

THE MARCH OUT OF EGYPT.

The march out of Egypt, as described by Moses, is pure fable, and, indeed, barefaced falsehood. In the first place, it would have required a master-mind to have directed such a movement, and we are not to suppose that Moses—who was guilty of writing such folly as the Bishop of Natal has proved, to at least his own satisfaction—could have been qualified for such a work.

Many persons, however, have differed with the Bishop of Natal on this point, and have believed that Moses was capable of having directed such a movement. And to this hour many persons are of this opinion. Moreover, those who think thus in opposition to Bishop Colenso are encouraged in their belief by the fact—that, from the days of Moses to the closing of the Canon of Holy Scripture, the inspired writers constantly referred to this march out of Egypt —and to the shepherd of the flock—to Moses—who was selected by God for that great work. And the Almighty knows how to not only select, but to fit His instruments for the work whereunto He calls them.

Nehemiah referred to this subject in his beautiful prayer. The Psalms make constant reference to it, as a foundation for more than common praise and thanksgiving to Almighty God. And in his lofty strains Isaiah breaks forth on the subject of this deliverance out of Egypt by the right hand of Moses. Jeremiah, too, and others of the Prophets, St. Stephen, and St. Paul,—all refer in one note of praise to God for this march out of Egypt under the guidance of Moses as the chosen and truly great leader of such a work. But, though all those sacred writers and high authorities referred to the march out of Egypt, as described by Moses in the selfsame words in which we read the account to this day, yet Bishop Colenso pronounces the statement as a fable and falsehood.

And, if there could remain a shadow of doubt as to this conclusion of the Bishop, that would be dispersed by this crowning proof that Moses did write falsehood on this point. These are the solemn words from which the Bishop draws this his unanswerable conclusion:—

"Remembering, as I do, the confusion in my own small household, of thirty or forty persons, when once we were obliged to fly at dead of night, having been roused from our beds with a false alarm that an invading Zulu force had entered the colony, had evaded the English troops sent to meet them, and was making its way direct for our Station, killing right and left as it came along—I do not hesitate to declare this statement to be utterly incredible and impossible." All which means, in plain language, that Moses wrote—for we must use again the terms—fable and falsehood to deceive mankind.

This must have been a very trying position in which the Bishop was placed by this "false alarm" and invasion—worse than our own French invasion—"and this killing right and left;" and we all know that false alarms, like imaginary ills, are far worse than real dangers, or positive sickness, to persons of certain minds, and to weak nerves.

But, allowing all this, and that Bishop Colenso, losing his head and presence of mind, "took to his heels," concluding with Falstaff that "discretion" was "the better part of valour;" though the Bishop might justify this rapid movement after the fashion of the Irishman, who, when taunted with having run away from the enemy, said, "My heart was in the right place, but it was those cowardly heels that made me run away"—now, we say, though all this be so, and, though the Bishop might thus justify the wisdom of Falstaff, or plead the apology of the Irishman, yet we cannot by any contrivance, or exercise of mind, find out how all this proves that Moses was a fool, and that he wrote fables on this subject, and that all the sacred writers and authorities conspired to give currency to such a tissue of absurdities and impossibilities.

But, although we cannot see the force of the conclusion against Moses drawn from the fright which Bishop Colenso experienced, and which made him trust more to his heels than to any other protection, yet there is one conclusion to which the Bishop leads, —in fact, drives us,—and that is, to quote the remark of George IV. in reference to a divine sent over by His

Majesty from England to an Irish See, and who was said to have run away because some Romanists served him with a notice to quit, headed with the sign of a death's head and cross bones, "That the bishop was not fit for the Church militant in Ireland." So we say that, apart from all other considerations, Bishop Colenso does not, by this story, prove himself to have been a fit soldier of the "Church militant" in Natal.

How very different the calm and commanding self-possession and courage of Nehemiah, who, when warned to flee because certain persons were coming down to slay him, " Yea, in the night they will come to slay thee," so nobly replied, "Should such a man as I flee?"

THE SHEEP AND CATTLE OF THE ISRAELITES IN THE DESERT.

This chapter of his objections the Bishop of Natal thus opens:—

"The *people*, we are told, were supplied with manna. But there was no miraculous provision for the herds and flocks. They were left to gather sustenance as they could in that inhospitable wilderness."

We have already, in our remarks on the animals in the ark, touched on the wonderful way in which a bountiful Creator supplies the wants of all His creatures.

We would now enlarge on the subject, not to reply to this foolish argument of Bishop Colenso, but because of the instruction which even his cavils suggest to the mind. We are not "told" how the cattle were fed, therefore they were left to starve! Are we "told" how the countless multitudes of the creatures of God are every day fed throughout the world? Not one word is uttered in the book of nature on this subject.

"The heavens declare the glory of God, and the firmament showeth His handywork."

How? Not in language. We are not "told" any thing. No. "There is neither speech nor language;" "but," for all that, "their voices are heard,"—heard by all nations. Thus, though the book of nature be dumb as to our not being "told" in so many words, yet is it most eloquent; and its voice is every where heard—heard in the fact that the creatures of God *are* under all circumstances supplied with daily sustenance. We may, then, justly pronounce such wretched cavilling as unworthy of serious notice.

But the consideration of the subject in its proper bearings will furnish profitable instruction, and will lift up the mind far above such poor sophistry as that of Bishop Colenso. We would, however, first remark, that we do not require extracts from any writers on the sand-storms, or such like phenomena, of those countries. Such subjects are very well known. And we all know that the whole land of promise has been little better than a waste and howling desert under the grinding domination of the Turkish rule;—as indeed it was foretold that the land should be desolate and trodden down, so as to be an object of remark and very scorn. All such quotation is, then, beside the question.

Cicero observed the difficulty of Bishop Colenso as to the way in which Nature sustained all creatures in all places, and with the very food suited to each—"qui cuique aptus erat." But Cicero observed this with wonder and admiration, and not to cavil and seek to prove the book of nature a fable, or to blot out from its pages the Providence of God. Seneca, too, has a fine sentence on this subject:—"It is God who has dispersed the herds throughout the whole world, and who provides food for the flocks which in all places roam at large." " Ille Deus est, qui per totum orbem armenta dimisit, qui gregibus ubique passim vagantibus pabulum præstat." Well said, noble heathen!

In the last great day, when the words and acts of men shall be disclosed, your sentiments will rise up in judgment against the flippant writings of many "philosophers of Christian times."

The provision which God makes for His creatures is thus described:—" These wait all upon Thee; that Thou mayst give them their meat in due season. That Thou givest them, they gather: Thou openest Thine hand, they are filled with good." And again:—" The eyes of all wait upon Thee, and Thou givest them their meat in due season. Thou openest Thine hand, and satisfiest the desire of every living thing." There may be trials for the animal creation, as well as for the race of man; but it was a great question which the Redeemer asked,—" Is not the life more than meat, and the body than raiment?"

Wherever the Almighty Father calls into existence any creature, He does not fail to provide for its wants. He, as has been beautifully said, " tempers the wind to the shorn lamb." Though Israel went through a wilderness, their great leader, at the close of his pilgrimage, could appeal unto them, that their raiment waxed not old, nor did their foot swell; and that their wants were all supplied. Where God gives the life, He gives what is necessary for its preservation. Where He forms the body, He finds ways to provide even raiment for the same. And, for the consolation of believers in His word, it may also be said, that, where He gives the promise of eternal life, He also provides food for that life, in the rich pastures of His promises, in "the means of grace," and " in the hope of glory."

"All this," as is well remarked in the words of the Christian philosopher already quoted, " affords us a glorious scene of the Divine Providence and management, which, as it concerns itself in lesser things, so we may presume, doth exert itself particularly in so grand an affair as that of food, whereby the animal world subsists.

"It is a great act of the Divine Power and Wisdom, as well as Goodness, to provide food for such a world of animals as every where possess the terraqueous globe. That the temperate climates, or at least the fertile valleys, and rich and plentiful regions of the earth, should afford subsistence to many animals, may appear less wonderful perhaps. But that in all other, the most unlikely places for supplies, sufficient food should be afforded to such a prodigious number, and so great variety of beasts, birds, fishes, and insects, is owing to that Being who hath as wisely adapted their bodies to their place and food, as well as carefully provided food for their subsistence there. Which Providence of God, particularly in the supplies afforded the *ravens*, is divers times taken notice of in the Scriptures. 'Who provideth for the raven his food? When his young ones cry unto God, they wander for lack of meat.' And 'He giveth to the beast his food, and to the young ravens which cry.' Thus our Saviour, too: 'Consider the ravens, for they neither sow nor reap, which neither have storehouse nor barn, and God feedeth them.' It is a manifest argument of the Divine Care and Providence in supplying the world with food and necessaries, that the *ravens*, accounted as unclean and little regarded by man, destitute of stores, and that live by accidents, by what falleth here and there; that such a bird, I say, should be provided with sufficient food; especially, if that be true which Aristotle, Pliny, and Ælian report of their unnatural affection and cruelty to their young, 'that they expel them from their nests as soon as they can fly, and then drive them out of the country.'"

Our author then thus concludes:—"And from this bare transient view of this branch of the great Creator's Providence and Government, relating to the food of His creatures, we can conclude no less than that, since this grand affair hath so manifest strokes of admirable and wise management; that since this is demonstrated throughout all ages and places, that, therefore, it is God's handywork. For, how is it possible that so vast a world of animals should be supported, such a great variety equally and well supplied with proper food in every place fit for habitation, without an especial superintendency and management, equal to, at least, that of the most prudent Steward and Householder[1]?"

And this Being, who thus presides over and directs such an amazing economy, who "crowns the year with His goodness" as with the most valuable diadem, and "whose paths drop fatness" even "*upon the pastures of the wilderness*," is the All-wise "God, THE FATHER ALMIGHTY," whose full and bountiful hand the Bishop of Natal would render so powerless by his arithmetic, and his cavils, and quotations about sand-storms, that THAT HAND should not dispense food to Its creatures, save only according to the notions and rules of Bishop Colenso!

CHAPTER XIII.

The invading army described by the Lion—All fable, according to Bishop Colenso—The Bishop's irreverent manner in speaking of the Word of God—His ludicrous argument to prove his case

---

[1] Derham's Boyle Lectures.

—Calculation of the Eastern Counties of England—His absurd mode of reasoning on this head—Only a subject for ridicule—The number of Priests—The minute calculations as to the time required for each duty—Many infidels would be ashamed to use Bishop Colenso's arguments—The true view of the Priest's duties—A question to the Bishop after his own way of arguing—On his principle, the history of England all fable—The war on Midian—The Bishop's mode of carrying off the captives—The numbers slain—Alleged cruelty of the Israelites—Nature and mystery of War—And of other elements of destruction—Used for the moral government of the world—The sun standing still—The words of Joshua do not necessarily maintain the Earth as centre of our system—Different views of Astronomers respecting even the spots on the Sun—The Creator, Master of His own laws—Mode in which the miracle is described might be correct—And yet not assert the Ptolemaic theory—Nature of the Sun—His motion and influence too little understood to justify the conclusion of infidels against the sacred writer.

NUMBER OF PEOPLE COMPARED WITH THE EXTENT OF CANAAN.

"He shall come up like a lion from the swelling of Jordan," is the grand imagery under which the Prophet describes the invading army.

The brow of the lion is so constructed, that it does not afford any protection from the glare of the sun. He cannot, therefore, endure its light; but, when "the sun ariseth, they get them to their dens; they lie down together." And man may then go "forth to his work and to his labour until the evening." We may then picture to our minds the fury of the lion, when, driven out of his lair by the swelling of Jordan, he roamed at large over the surrounding country. But this is all a mistake; the whole of this imagery is founded on mere fable. There were not, and could not have been, any lions in the land of Judea. And this Bishop Colenso proves as a fact.

The Bishop quotes the passage where the Almighty states that He would drive out the Hivites, Canaanites, and Hittites from before the seed of Abraham, to whom the promise of the land was made. For the wickedness of those nations did the Lord drive them out; and such was that wickedness, that it is said that, because of it, the land vomited them out. But the Almighty says, by His servant Moses, in the words quoted by the Bishop, " I will not drive them out from before thee in one year, lest the land become desolate, and the beast of the field multiply against thee. By little and little I will drive them out from before thee, until thou be increased, and inherit the land."

We shall not stop to dwell on the wisdom, and the consideration for the children of Israel, which is contained in this policy. But Bishop Colenso takes a very different view of the question, and shows the whole statement to be an utter impossibility, and a barefaced falsehood.

This the Bishop of Natal proves by his recourse to his figures—square miles, acres—statistics, and such like arguments. He informs us, in the first place, that the utmost extent of the land of promise was so many square miles, and so many acres; and this he proves as one of his facts.

Having, then, proved all this calculation to be " the truth," the Bishop adds, " and, according to this story, this was occupied by more than two millions of people." The "story," at which this Christian Bishop thus scoffs, is the passage of Holy Scripture recorded as the very words of the God of Truth!!!

The Bishop then enters into another learned calculation, founded on the size of the counties of Norfolk, Suffolk, and Essex; and he gives the statistics of those counties according to the census of 1850. And then, having assumed the impossibility of the land of Canaan containing such a population, he proves further that it was impossible, because of the aboriginal Canaanites who already filled the land;—" seven nations," quotes the Bishop, "*greater* and *mightier* than Israel itself."

The italics, "*greater and mightier,*" are the property of Bishop Colenso. This stress on those words is merely the mode of Bishop Colenso; a way of his own to make Moses contradict himself; as if Moses did not know what he wrote, but required the learned instructions and petty calculations of the Bishop of Natal.

The Bishop then thus rises higher and higher in his *sorites:* "And surely it cannot be said that these three Eastern Counties, with their flourishing towns, Norwich, Lynn, Yarmouth," and seventeen other towns, and the "&c." which the Bishop names, "and their innumerable villages, are in any danger of lying 'desolate,' with the beasts of the field multiplying against the human inhabitants."

For the sake of the landlords, and farmers, and all who are dependent on their noble toil, we most sincerely sympathize with the Bishop's remarks, and trust that there is not any danger of such "desolation." And as to " the beasts of the field multiplying against the human inhabitants,"—and we would include the cattle of those fertile counties with their flourishing towns and their innumerable villages,—we most devoutly hope, for the sake of the people, that there is not the least danger of such a fearful contingency. And we as devoutly hope, that the inhabitants will not feel any ground for alarm from the bare idea of such an event as that which Bishop Colenso suggests, in order to overthrow the truth of the Word of God! An invasion of the Eastern Counties by lions, wolves, and hyenas! the idea is dreadful, and may have a most depressing effect on many important interests.

"Sed tamen amoto quæramus seria ludo."

Although, as Horace says,

"—— quanquam ridentem dicere verum
Quid vetat?"

We may speak much truth in a merry mood.

The Bishop then proceeds to the climax of his argument. He shows the extent of the colony of Natal. The population, he admits, is scanty. Yet the inhabitants are able to maintain their ground against the beasts of the field. The lion, elephant, and other animals, have long ago disappeared, and in his travels the Bishop never saw one.

And, therefore, all this cumulative evidence proves that the statement put into the words of the Almighty by His servant Moses, is all pure invention and falsehood, sent abroad for some wicked purpose; but what that wicked purpose was, is not stated by Bishop Colenso.

Now, reader, if you can connect the conclusion of the Bishop of Natal with such extraordinary premises, you will do something beyond the powers of other men.

"THE NUMBER OF PRIESTS AT THE EXODUS COMPARED WITH THEIR DUTIES, AND WITH THE PROVISION MADE FOR THEM."

Such is the title of another of the Bishop's arguments against the truth of the Pentateuch. The Bishop gives in detail the duties of the priesthood; and then, in these words, challenges the whole race of fools who would still persist in their belief in the Pentateuch, as a part of the revelation of a merciful Creator to the lost race of man:

"And now let me ask, for all those multifarious duties during the forty years' sojourn in the wilderness, — for all the burnt-offerings, meat-offerings, peace-offerings, sin-offerings, trespass-offerings, thank-offerings, of a population like that of the City of LONDON, besides the daily and extraordinary sacrifices—how many priests were there?"

He would be a wonderful man who, at this time of day, would venture to answer this question. But the Bishop does not leave us in doubt. "The answer," he says, "is very simple." "There were only *three*,— Aaron" (till his death) "and his two sons, Eleazar and Ithamar." "And," the Bishop continues, "it is laid down solemnly in N. iii. 10, 'Thou shalt appoint Aaron and his sons, and they shall wait in the priest's office, and the stranger that cometh nigh shall be put to death.'" And then the Bishop thus proceeds:—
"Yet how was it possible that these two or three men should have discharged all these duties for such a vast multitude? The single work, of offering the double offering for women after childbirth, must have utterly overpowered three priests, though engaged without cessation from morning to night."

We are very sorry indeed to break the thread of this learned argument of Bishop Colenso; but we feel a something within which compels us to bow to truth, and express our sincere and hearty concurrence with this important question.

Reader, only think of the Bishop of London's position, if, in addition to his lordship's morning correspondence, his levees, his reception of deputations, his duties as a peer of the realm, his ordinations, consecrations, confirmations, preaching, lecturing, attendance at meetings, and the vast amount of work besides—not to speak of some little allowance for taking food and rest—for his lordship is, after all, only a mortal, and must feed on something more than air!—now only think of the Bishop having, in addition to such work, to church all the women after childbirth who may happen to reside within his lordship's diocese! This would, in the words of the Bishop of Natal, "utterly overpower" his lordship, "though engaged without cessation from morning to night."

We believe Bishop Colenso on this point at least. Such work would overpower his Lordship of London. And we sincerely hope that, if the Bishop of Natal and his friends succeed in publishing a new Bible, and in establishing a new Church, they will pause before they impose on their Bishop of London any such "overpowering" duties. Indeed, the mere churching of the women of London after childbirth would, independently of any other duty, "utterly overpower him;" not to state that in fact the light of the moon would have to be as the light of the sun, and the light of the sun not only sevenfold, but seventy times sevenfold, for such daily work.

The Bishop then goes on to his arithmetic. "We can scarcely," he writes, "allow less than *five minutes* to each sacrifice;"—he had before *proved* two hundred and fifty to be the number of births each day, which would have involved, for the two, the burnt-offering and the sin-offering, five hundred sacrifices; and those sacrifices would have taken two thousand five hundred minutes; and two thousand five hundred minutes would be nearly forty-two hours; and, therefore, " could not have been offered in a single day of twelve hours, though each of the three priests had been employed in the one incessant labour of offering them" (that is, the mere offerings for the women), "without a moment's rest or intermission."

We can only say of this last sentence of the Bishop as Juvenal said of Cicero—

" O, si sic omnia!"

If in all other points the Bishop had spoken as much truth, he would have bid fair to have converted a world. It is, indeed, a self-evident proposition. But it was a work of mere supererogation to have gone into such a display of arithmetic, for every one must subscribe to the statement, that such an amount of work "must have utterly overpowered three priests, though engaged without cessation from morning to night."

But the fact is, that, after all, though we bow with much reverence to the "truth," as in this instance stated by Bishop Colenso, yet we cannot see that Moses was a fool, and an inventor of fables and lies; and that, therefore, Christianity is itself but fable. We cannot connect such self-evident premises with the conclusion of the Bishop. And we are satisfied that there are many infidels who would be ashamed to use such despicable arguments against the Revelation of God.

Now, without any reference to the Bishop of Natal, we always understood the plain common-sense view of the question;—that Aaron was the head of the priesthood, and that any person not "called of God as was Aaron," who attempted to usurp the sacred office, was guilty of an offence, punishable with death. "The stranger that cometh nigh shall be put to death;" for such a person would be guilty of not only an act of high treason against the law, but against the Almighty

Himself, whose direct appointment and command such usurper would set at defiance.

This the history of Korah, Dathan, and Abiram proved. And on this ground Moses asked Korah, the ringleader in that rebellion, " And what is Aaron, that ye murmur against him?" Aaron is only the appointed head of the priesthood, selected and appointed by Jehovah; therefore you are not guilty of rebellion against Aaron, but against God Himself.

But Aaron had a whole tribe under him to minister in the various offices of the priesthood.

"And the Lord spake unto Moses, saying, Bring the tribe of Levi near." How—we might by the way ask, on the principle of the Bishop, so curiously calculated in another place—how could a whole tribe have been brought near? " And present them before Aaron the priest, that they may minister unto him. And they shall keep his charge, and the charge of the whole congregation before the Tabernacle of the Congregation, to do the service of the Tabernacle. And thou shalt give the Levites unto Aaron and to his sons: they are wholly given unto him out of the children of Israel."

And when Moses blessed the tribes, he showed more particularly the duties of the tribe of Levi. " They shall teach Jacob Thy judgments, and Israel Thy law: they shall put incense before Thee, and whole burnt sacrifice upon Thine altar."

So we see that there was some provision made against the alarming contingency of Bishop Colenso; and that Aaron was not abandoned to be so "utterly overpowered, though engaged without cessation from morning to night." And Moses, when he wrote this account of the duties of the priesthood, was not such a fool and tyrant as the Bishop of Natal would have us believe.

Aaron, then, is named merely as head or sovereign of the order, in whose family the high priesthood descended as an inheritance.

St. Paul was of this mind. He puts Aaron as head or representative of the Jewish priesthood, as Christ is the head of the unchangeable priesthood, or the priesthood that was not to pass to others, but to remain His who was the great High Priest for ever after the order of Melchisedec.

And, in another place, St. Paul writes to show, that the tribe, of which Aaron was the head, had the priesthood as their right and portion. "And, verily, they that are of the tribe of Levi who receive the office of the priesthood, have a commandment to take tithes of the people according to the law."

Now, as the Bishop of Natal is so fond of assuming extravagant cases in order to prove Moses a fool and wilful deceiver; and, in reference to this question, asks—How was it possible that Aaron, the only high priest (in his lifetime),—as the Bishop writes,—even if assisted by his two sons,—how was it possible that he could have performed so many duties every day, when the mere daily work of the sacrifices on behalf of the women alone, if performed even by three priests, would have occupied very many days, and therefore could not have been performed in twelve hours — even if only five minutes had been allowed to each sacrifice?

Now we will put our question. Are we then to suppose, or could it have been tolerated, that the whole tribe of Levi, which was thus separated for the work of the priesthood, should have spent their lives like so many monks, or idle drones, living on the tithes, and not doing any thing but looking from day to day at Aaron toiling beyond endurance, if engaged only in the matter of the women after childbirth, to which the Bishop has applied his minute and learned calculations?

We might as well take the case of our Sovereign Lady Queen Victoria, and calculate, first, the almost countless millions of her glorious empire on which the sun never goes down; and then the amount of duty which our Sovereign has to discharge every day, and which is discharged in her name, and as her act. And, we may add, that if any person were to come nigh, and seek to usurp the right to discharge those duties, that person would be put to death as guilty of high treason, the highest crime known in law. And whereas the Bishop allows that Aaron's two sons might have assisted him, the law of England does not allow any partner in the rights of the Sovereign.

And now to apply the Bishop's mode of arguing. Yet how was it possible that one queen should discharge all those duties for such almost countless millions? The single work of daily correspondence with such a multitude must "utterly overpower her, though engaged without cessation from morning to night." Why, if you allow only one minute for each letter, the work of a day would require many months, and as that work which would require months could not be performed in twelve hours, therefore, reader, the whole history of England, laws, constitution and all, are mere idle tales!

THE WAR ON MIDIAN.

The last of the objections of Bishop Colenso against the truth of the Pentateuch is "the war on Midian." In this chapter the old arguments of infidels of past days are reproduced by the Bishop, with, at the same time, one very original idea as to the impossibility of 12,000 Israelites "having carried off 100,000 captives," which the Bishop very justly remarks would have been more than eight captives to each man.

And, if by "carried off" we are to understand that the Israelites actually carried the captives on their backs, then we should be very much inclined to think that the Bishop is right; and that eight captives and a decimal point or piece of the four captives—which would be the surplus over the hundred multiplied by twelve,—that, we say, eight and a decimal point of four captives would have been too heavy a burden for one man, especially if that man had to carry a tent and other "cumbrous articles" referred to in a former chapter.

But yet the Irish soldier took several prisoners, and, when praised by his commander for the act, and asked how he managed such an exploit, replied, "Plaise your honour, I surrounded them!" Well, 12,000 could better have surrounded the 100,000 captives than one Irishman could have surrounded three or four prisoners of war. This idea, on which a further and grand objection against the Pentateuch is founded, is, we repeat, quite original. At least, in the course of our reading, we never met with it before. We need not waste time in proving that large bodies have laid down their arms to a mere handful of men, and have marched before them as captives.

The two leading points, however, in this stale objection are the number reported as slain, and the cruelty of the Israelites. As to the reported number of slain the Bishop goes into a most minute calculation, and shows that only so many were slain at Waterloo, and that, therefore, no more than the exact proportion which he will allow could have been slain in the war on Midian.

We all know that the advance in the science of war has, in a measure, humanized warfare, and made less the destruction of mankind. When the vultures in the parable of Johnson held a consultation as to what beings were their best friends, they unanimously decided that, beyond all comparison, man was that best friend.

We read in history of a few individuals from age to age having been killed by a lion, or a tiger, or a bear, or a wolf; but countless millions of men have been slain by their fellow-men. What comparison, then, between the tribe of lions, and the race of man, as friends to the vulture? Therefore George III. well replied to Watson's repudiation of any compliment on his improvement in gunpowder, "A sorry subject, your Majesty, on which to compliment a Christian bishop;" "Not at all, sir; any thing which tends to mitigate the horrors of war is a very proper subject of compliment to any man."

In former days wars were vastly more destructive than they are now. Read Homer, and see the havoc which Diomede made where the poet describes him as armed with a commission and assistance from some of the gods to destroy the Trojans. Homer was a poet, and some licence is given to poets as well as to travellers; but, after all, Homer's description of the terrible slaughter by even one man was founded on the fact that the most powerful, like, as Horace remarks, the bull in the herd, dealt out death at pleasure.

This was the natural consequence of the mode of warfare in those days, when each man selected his man, and when the weaker, as a matter of mere necessity, succumbed to the more powerful foe. And when Alexander, Hannibal, and Scipio contended for precedence before the bar of Minos in the lower regions, Alexander, in reply to Hannibal's statement of his exploits, says, "Indeed, Minos, it would appear to be useless to reply to such a self-confident man, but the whole world knows what a robber he was, and what a great man and conqueror I was." And in reference to the number which he slew, he appeals to Minos and the whole staff of officers in Hades, " I need not to speak; you all know my exploits, and how I bridged up the rivers with the dead, and sent down such multitudes to you in one day, that the boat of Charon was utterly insufficient for its purpose, and you had to construct rafts to carry over the shades of the slain."

We often laughed in days gone by at the wit of the writer in whose pages this account is to be found, but we little thought that we should ever have had those passages occur to the mind to reprove a Christian bishop for his absurd writing, and wicked attack on the Revelation of God.

But yet all this wit, at the expense of the folly of mankind in thinking of such questions even after their departure from this world, is founded on the fact that in those days warfare was fearfully and almost incredibly destructive in its effects; but since war has become more a science, and the means of destruction more terrible, the pigmy is a match for the giant, and the slaughter of the human race has been greatly reduced.

And yet Bishop Colenso enters into his usual calculations, and states the number of the slain on the field of Waterloo; and, fixing on that number as the standard which is to regulate all modes of warfare and all ages, past, present, and to come, on such laughable grounds concludes that the record of salvation is a fable—for all parts of that record must stand or fall together. It is not a record of Bishop Colenso's devising; and we have yet to discover, in other ways than by his pretensions, the Bishop of Natal's competence, in respect to his wisdom or learning, to set aside the record of salvation by any such silly application of his arithmetic.

As to the cruelty of the Israelites; "the horrors of war" would be a better term. When once the sword is unsheathed, who can control its destructive power?

When once men "cry havoc, and let slip the dogs of war," who can regulate their infuriated passions? And, if this be the natural result of war under any circumstances, how much more was it not so under the old system of warfare?

When the Almighty, after having created all things, established the laws of nature, which we call "the fixed laws," and which are so fixed only by His appointment, He reserved in His own hands certain elements for the moral government of the world: those elements to be, as they are to this day, used for that purpose under His superintending Providence.

Amongst the chief of those elements are the sword, the famine, and the pestilence; we have, besides, earthquakes, lightnings, and tempests doing their terrible work of correction and judgment on sea and land. But the sword, the famine, and the pestilence, with the noisome beast mentioned in the sacred writings, all make up "my four sore judgments," saith the Lord God Almighty.

Now, as we have said in the case of slavery, the revelation of God did not create war. The very heathen can inform us on this point. How is the revelation of God accountable for this terrible scourge? It, in common with the book of nature, only deals with war as with famine, pestilence, and other destructive elements, as facts, as instruments used by God for the punishment of the guilty, and not only guilty, but in too many instances actively wicked, race of man.

The heathen world represented their father of gods and men, Jupiter, as every moment, on the slightest provocation, hurling his thunderbolt at the heads of bad men. When Jupiter was sending Mercury on some special message, he called him back, and said, "And, when you are on your return, call in at Ætna and have my thunderbolt sharpened; for it was blunted lately, when I shot it at that villain of a philosopher, who was teaching the people that there were no gods, but the fellow stooped his head, and the thunderbolt struck on a rock, and its points were blunted; but call in and have it sharpened, and I'll have a shot at those fellows who have treated Timon in such an infamous way." For Mercury had told Jupiter how Timon's friends had sucked the very marrow out of his bones; and then, when they had got all out of him, neglected him in the most ungrateful and insolent manner.

The heathen world had not the light of that glorious revelation which Bishop Colenso would, if he could, cause to set in "blackness of darkness for ever," and substitute his farthing rushlight in its place; and, therefore, we need not wonder that even the learned Greeks believed much of what their satirist thus lashes with severity.

But, unlike the Jupiter of the heathen world, the Almighty Creator and Ruler of the Universe is slow in His proceedings against an unthankful and rebellious race. "Long-suffering" is one of the parts of His great and glorious name; and, as an old divine said, "it cost Him more pains to destroy Jericho than create the world." He governs by established laws, and not by judgments instigated by passion; and He makes sinners to chastise themselves, that they may know in their hearts "what an evil and bitter thing it is to have departed from the living God."

Thus the Creator acts in a calm and dignified manner in all His judgments, and by this way stops every mouth, and brings in the whole world as guilty before Him; men being compelled to acknowledge that they have brought their judgments upon themselves.

And whether we refer to the "war on Midian," or any wars, it is just the same. The commission is, "Sword, go through the land." Read the nature of war, not in the history of the battle-field, but in the consequences of the battle; or read the history of the siege of some great town, not in the mere fighting, but in the letting loose the unbridled passions of an infuriated soldiery, when, after they take by storm a place that has refused to surrender, and which has therefore caused a vast destruction of human life, such soldiery are let loose for a given number of days to sack the unhappy town. "Death would be chosen rather than life" by the residue of those that would survive the actual siege.

Thus the result is the same, whether we read it in words, as in the history of the "war on Midian," or in the mere facts; and the one as much as the other is a part of the government of God. It is a sad thing that the innocent should in such cases suffer, but they do in all such cases suffer; and the fact that they will suffer may sometimes lead men to pause, before they bring about such dreadful consequences.

But innocent children to the third and fourth generation suffer because of the wicked lives of their fathers; and poor babes are involved in the same destruction in all the accidents of "flood and field," and every day numbers of innocent persons are involved in ruin—ruin to descend to their latest posterity—by the designing villainy of their fellow-men; and such villains prosper for a time—often a long time. And this fact has in all ages quite perplexed the minds of most sincere believers in the good Providence of God.

In the Psalms, the Prophets, and other parts of Holy Writ, this state of things has been a sore trial to the people of God, which they confessed themselves unable to solve; and had only to stay themselves on the word of Abraham, "Shall not the Judge of all the earth do right?"

And even heathen writers, referring to this difficulty in the government of the world, sought the explanation almost in the words of the sacred writer, "Surely Thou didst set them in slippery places." When speaking of the prosperity of actually wicked men, Charon is made to exclaim in some such words as these: "Well done, noble Clotho; lift them up the higher, that their fall may be the heavier, and may afford more cause of rejoicing at their deserved end."

We ask then, once again, are we, poor finite beings, worms of the dust, to challenge the Almighty Ruler of the Universe, and call Him to account for this His mode of administration of His own affairs; or turn upon Him, and revile and blaspheme His Word—whether spoken in words in the book of grace, or in acts in the book of nature, because these such painful trials of our faith and patience are thus recorded in those volumes?

These, as we have already said, these are the trials of faith; and not the laughable difficulties of the size of court-yards, cleansing of camps, and carriage of tents by oxen, "if they had been trained as pack-oxen!"

These are, indeed, the difficulties and trials in this world of time, which can only be—but which will be—cleared up in that future state to which we are all hastening; and, we may say, difficulties, which, if they were to be exhibited to our view in the morning of life, would paralyze all exertion, and consign us to a drivelling existence to the very evening of our days. How Shakespeare has treated this idea—

> "O heaven! that one might read the book of fate;
> And see the revolution of the times
> Make mountains level, and the continent
> (Weary of solid firmness) melt itself
> Into the sea! and, other times, to see
> The beachy girdle of the ocean
> Too wide for Neptune's hips: how chances mock,
> And changes fill the cup of alteration
> With divers liquors! O if this were seen,
> The happiest youth,—viewing his progress through,
> What perils past, what crosses to ensue,—
> Would shut the book, and sit him down and die."

These, and such like dispensations, are the difficulties which, though they do not make all men infidels, are the real trials which shake faith, and which bring forth from some—"Though He slay me, yet will I trust in Him."

THE SUN STANDING STILL.

Having examined, with two or three exceptions, so many of the worn-out objections of Bishop Colenso to the Pentateuch; objections which the Bishop and his band of followers imagine will sweep the fable of Moses from the land, we conclude our weary task with some notice of the well-known one in the book of Joshua, to which the Bishop refers in his preface. We have said "weary task;" for such indeed the examination of Bishop Colenso's volume has been. We do not desire to give offence; but we write as an independent thinker:

> "Nullius addictus jurare in verba magistri."

And as Bishop Colenso has so freely stated his opinion, that the writings of Moses are fable and folly, we think that we, as believers in that part and parcel of the revelation of our Creator, and as of the same mind with the Apostle of the Gentiles, " If in this life only we have hope in Christ, we are of all men most miserable," have also a right to state our view of his book. We have, besides, now to bear every kind of reproach, and vain babblings far worse than reproach, wherever we go, because a number of men whose only motto is—" Rem, recte si possis, sed quocunque modo rem," "Money at all hazards, at the cost of heaven itself," have been stirred up in a wonderful manner to defend glaring infidelity, and whose God and Bible are the Bishop of Natal and his infidel book.

Now we think this a very hard case. For ourselves, we have never trespassed on the "loaves and fishes" of the Church; and we therefore come forward as merely a solitary individual of the professing Christians of the land—" unus multorum," " one of the million,"—and " paullo infirmior," perhaps, than our new philosophers; one of those weak persons who think that Moses was not a fool or a deceiver; and that the Revelation of God, from the first chapter of Genesis to the last chapter of the book of the Revelation, has been, beyond all comparison, the greatest blessing which a merciful Creator ever bestowed upon the fallen and heavily afflicted race of man.

With such feelings, then, we claim the right to use as much candour in speaking of the production of Bishop Colenso, as he does in speaking of the writings of Moses. Therefore we repeat that the perusal of his volume has been a weary work. The task reminds us of the remarks of Horace, when advised not to write any more,—" May I perish, my good father, but your advice is good; but I cannot sleep unless I write."

"Let those," replied his friend, "who require sound sleep, anoint their bodies and swim several times across the Tiber."

Well, we can prescribe a better remedy for those who require sleep, and who have ever studied the questions on which Bishop Colenso writes. Let them read and work out the arithmetic of Bishop Colenso, by which he would prove the Word of God a fable, and they will not have any need of the prescription of Horace.

We now examine the objections founded on the words of Joshua, "Sun, stand thou still." We have had for very many years a view of this question, which has satisfied our mind that Joshua never thought of contradicting the now established philosophy on this subject; and that too many persons have concluded, without sufficient grounds, that Joshua spoke what was philosophically untrue. We do not care to notice Bishop Colenso, who serves up the old objections of shallow infidels. There are two points in this question: the first, whether any thing of the kind could have occurred, or ever did occur; and, secondly, the mode of speech in which the fact is described.

We suppose that few persons, except those of most depraved minds, those "fools" who say "in their hearts there is no God;" and the word "fools" does not mean men of weak intellect, but deliberately wicked men, who use hand and tongue against the Most High; now we not only suppose, but conclude that none but such would assert that the Creator is so bound down, or such a slave to any laws established by Himself in His own universe, as that He could not, without an effort, suspend, alter, or abrogate any of those laws.

The heathen world believed that their deities were in abject subjection to fate; but not so with Him Who is the "Maker of Heaven and earth, and of all things visible and invisible." If this be admitted, then the causing not merely the sun, but the universe itself, to stand still would not cost an effort, and could not be attended with any, even the least, inconvenience to His creatures.

We know all the theories and calculations as to the way in which we and all bodies on this earth, for instance, would be hurled into space, if the earth were to be suddenly stopped in its journey. But all this is mere fallacy; it has a show of reason,—but a mere show,—and is only folly in the extreme. We shall not, therefore, labour to prove that the Creator of the universe can suspend His own laws without the permission of Bishop Colenso; or without making the mode of suspension depend on the arithmetic of the Bishop of Natal.

It may, however, be well to mention, that, as in the case of the deluge, to which we have referred as not having been invented by Moses, so, in this instance, we may observe that the heathen world had some account,—we say some, for the obscurity of the account is not the question; that would be the natural consequence of a tradition passing down from age to age,—that, we say, the heathen world had some account of this very matter. We quote what is to persons of any reading a well-known passage, but what may be interesting to others, as showing that some such circumstances as those described in the history of Joshua, and again in the history of Hezekiah, were not only believed in the heathen world, but were recorded in the chronicles of the Egyptians, to whose country all men repaired to obtain knowledge.

After referring to other information which he obtained from the Egyptians, Herodotus, who wrote five hundred years before the Christian Era, says, "But during this time they asserted that four times the sun had risen out of his usual seats; and that twice he rose where he now sets; and that twice he set where he now rises. They add that, in consequence of these revolutions, no alterations in regard to Egypt, whether land or river, occurred, nor likewise with respect to diseases, or the things pertaining to death."

This statement, Herodotus says, the priests of Jupiter showed him. Therefore, although we shall not insult our readers with any attempt at proof that the Creator can control the works of His own hands, we have given this account of the tradition which obtained in the world as to some very extraordinary phenomena in the rising and setting of the sun.

The question then is,—not as to the power of the Creator to have produced such a very wonderful result, as the lengthening of the day in the history of Joshua, nor yet as to the fact; for, independently of the history of the fact in the Book of Joshua, we have that fact referred to as known, however confusedly, to the heathen world. The only subject in debate, then, except with avowed infidels, who deny the possibility, probability, or fact of a revelation from God to man, is the way in which the miracle is described in the Book of Joshua, "Sun, stand thou still."

We pass by any explanation founded on the language used to this very day of the sun rising and going down, which is, and must be, the common language of all mankind. We remember a quaint remark of an old divine, in an explanation of some parable, where, in speaking of the fanciful views which some men took of the mere phraseology in which the instruction was conveyed, says, "Note well, the words of a parable must not be squeezed too much, or we may extract blood, not milk."

And we pass by the explanation of commentators,

who plead for Joshua that he was not commissioned to teach astronomy, and that, if he had spoken to the people in any other words, or in strictly scientific language, he would not have been understood, and that, therefore, he adopted the commonly received notion that the sun went round the earth,—in fact, the now exploded system of Ptolemy, that the earth was the centre of our system, with the sun and planets revolving around this little speck in creation. But it is not said that Joshua spake any thing to the people. He showed them the result,—the miraculous interposition of God on their behalf. Joshua spake to God, and then gave his command to the sun, and also to the moon. "Then spake Joshua to the LORD in the day when the Lord delivered up the Amorites before the children of Israel, and he said in the sight of Israel, Sun, stand thou still upon Gibeon; and thou, Moon, in the valley of Ajalon."

We have always believed that it will yet be discovered, that, as in the case of some points of philosophy propounded by Moses, and referred to in a former chapter, Joshua did speak in more accurate language than men generally suppose. Is there, we ask, even at this day, an astronomer on the face of the earth who can state beyond possibility of doubt, or question, the nature of the sun? or of the exact nature of his influence on the whole, or on any part, of the system over which he presides?

Nay, take not merely the sun itself, but take the spots on the sun, and begin with the inventor of the telescope, or perhaps, rather, the first man who constructed one for practical purposes, and come down to our own Sir J. Herschel, or any of our modern astronomers, and, we boldly ask, is there one man amongst them who can pretend to so explain the mere spots on the surface of the sun, as to make the rejection of his views a ground for such an unerring conclusion as that any contrary view would be only a fable and a lie?

What Seneca said must be, and actually is, the confession of all our really great men. We must confess that we do not know any thing as we ought to know, —not that we are inferior in intellect to men of former ages, but that time is the great teacher of man. And, as Seneca says, "The people of the next age shall know many things unknown to us: many are reserved for ages then to come, when we shall be quite forgotten. The world would be a pitiful small thing, indeed, if it did not contain enough for the inquiries of the whole world." And again, "Much work still remains, and much will remain; neither to him that shall be born after a thousand ages will matter be wanting for new additions to what hath already been invented."

Now, then, if this be so, yet, if we differ from others or others from us, we do not see that their view, or our view, could entitle any of us to draw such a conclusion as that such view was to overthrow the Revelation of God.

But, if what we assert as to the readily acknowledged ignorance on the part of our greatest astronomers as to the nature, and the whole of the effects, or influence, of the sun on any, or all, of the planets over which he presides, be true, then how can any man pretend to lay down his opinion as premises, from which to draw the conclusion that the Book of Joshua stated what was contrary to what "we know to be the truth," as our self-styled philosophers would say? "And therefore it is quite evident that that portion of the so-called Revelation of God is mere fable. In fact, we have weighed the whole question in the balance of reason,"— that is, reader, *their own* reason,—and you must not, in the least degree, doubt that reason and *their* reason are one and the same Divine gift.

But where, we may ask, does the Book of Joshua ever assert that the earth is the centre of our system, and that the sun and planets revolve around this little speck in creation?

The now received idea of the sun being the centre and life of our system is not new. It was declared by Pythagoras 500 years before the birth of Christ. And who can say what was known or even recorded before the time of Pythagoras? The destruction of the Alexandrian library has left the world in much uncertainty as to what was written in its earlier ages.

But if Pythagoras laid down the Copernican theory that the sun, and not the earth, is the centre of our system, who, we repeat, can pronounce with any degree of certainty, or pronounce at all, what was known on this subject before the time of that philosopher? He, however, appears to have thought in advance of his day, and to have anticipated the discoveries of modern times. So his theory fell to the ground, and, up to the time of Copernicus, the notion prevailed that the earth is the centre of our system, and that around it the sun and planets revolve.

This notion is now exploded. Modern discoveries have proved the contrary. But, because the sun does not move round the earth as its centre, has not, therefore, the sun any motion of his own? If the old idea were the true view, then we believe that Joshua would have spoken in a different way, and would have said to earth as the centre of life and motion, " Earth, stand thou still."

There is a unity of design and harmony in all the works of God. Acting on this truth, the Apostle of the Gentiles reasons from the nature of this microcosm, the human body, in favour of sympathy with, and dependency on the other, of all the members of the Church of Christ. And, if we adopt the illustration, then we say that, if we want to bring to a stand any member or part of this little world, the body of man, we need not trouble ourselves about dealing with such member, or part, or parts, of the human system; which mode, after all, would only produce irregular and convulsive movements; like the earth, before a volcanic eruption, when it throws off every thing from its surface, as with violent movement it reels " to and fro, and staggers like a drunken man."

There is a much shorter way of attaining the object in view, and of accomplishing it in the best manner. Let us address ourselves to the centre of life and motion of this little world, the heart, and all is done in a moment, and in the most certain, noiseless, and effective way.

Now with the sun our whole system sympathizes, if we may so speak; and on his influence the life and motion of that system depends; and, therefore, were we to be commissioned, by any intimation from the Almighty Creator of the Universe, to demand such a result, we should have acted and spoken just as Joshua did; and we believe that thus the end desired would have been brought about in the easiest way.

We give our view with all humility and deference to the opinion of others, and not as "the truth," which is to overthrow all else. But where all is opinion and conjecture as to the nature of the sun, or even of its mere accidentals, and full influence, we humbly hope that we shall not be considered as if we meant to dogmatize, or in any way make light of the views of other men.

Our chief object is to show the impossibility of

laying down as certain, premises founded on such uncertainty in the world of opinion; and then, contrary to all principles of sound reasoning, drawing from such uncertainties the positive conclusion, that we ourselves are the only wise. We think our view sustained by the fact recorded, that the Moon also stood still. What had the moon to do with the lengthening of day? the moon was appointed to rule over and govern the night; and all this Joshua knew. The Earth and the Sun were alone concerned in bringing about such a result as the lengthening of the day. And yet it is written, that in answer to the command of Joshua to the Moon, to stand still in the valley of Ajalon, " and the Moon stayed."

Who then, we recur to the question, can state the exact nature of the Sun, and the full extent and operations of his influence on this our system, arising from merely his revolution on his own axis? And who can state with unerring certainty the exact nature of his work, and influence on the subjects of his world, as he travels through the unbounded region of space, attended by his magnificent court; and revolving with incredible speed around a far more distant Sun, his Divinely appointed Sovereign Lord, and centre of life and motion?

We are, in truth, but mere children in knowledge. And it is a reversal of the order of nature to put forth the folly of childhood as the wisdom of age; and, to go the step farther, and attempt to correct the wisdom of the Infinitely Wise—whether written in the Book of Nature or of Revelation—by such folly of childhood, is the climax of ignorance, impiety, and vain conceit.

Therefore, to conclude. We must admit, that the Creator of the Universe can do with His own creation and laws as He will; that, apart from His interference, such an event as that under consideration would have been impossible; and that, if done by His command, the event must have been done in the best and most easy way. And, reasoning from analogy, we may, we think, conclude that the mode of accomplishment is, at least, not so improperly described; as if, because Joshua assumed that the sun has a motion of his own, he therefore said that such motion is round the earth.

And, we may further conclude, that our imperfect knowledge on this, or on any subject in the world of Nature, does not justify the assumption of superior wisdom and veracity on the part of Bishop Colenso; and certainly not justify his poor and impious conclusion, that the Sacred Writings—the Revelation of God—are a fable and a lie.

CHAPTER XIV.

Review of Bishop Colenso's two modes of arguing against the Sacred Writers—The line which the Bishop should adopt to set aside the Inspired Records—What the principles of the Bishop's school would establish in place of the Bible—"Inconveniences from a proposed abolition of Christianity" recommended to modern reformers of the Bible—Christianity not a mere code of precepts—The light of nature from God—Gives birth to noble sentiments—But cannot teach the way of peace—The light of nature not what the Bishop's work would substitute for the Bible—The "Age of Reason" is the substitute of his school—First disciple of the Age of Reason—His act and doctrine contrasted with acts and doctrines from the light of nature—Terrible effects of the establishment of the Age of Reason in France—Appeal to the reader.

In the preceding chapters, we have endeavoured to carry out the title of our volume—"The Pretensions of Bishop Colenso to impeach the wisdom and veracity of the compilers of the Sacred Writings considered." We have tried by the rules of reasoning and common sense his principles of arguing against the inspired records, and have showed that, by proving too much, the Bishop of Natal proves nothing; or, to otherwise state the question, proves that there is not any thing in existence capable of being proved, if objections and cavils are to take the place of positive evidence, and be used to overthrow all records sacred and profane, because there may be found, in such records, some things which we do not understand or approve.

Such a line of argument against the Inspired writings, or against any writings, or any subject placed before the mind, carries its own refutation; and must prove how little knowledge of the real nature of mathematics or logic any man must possess who could descend to, and use, such a wretched system of cavilling, and then expect men to receive the same as proof deduced from the sound exercise of reason.

This is the first step in the mode of argument adopted by Bishop Colenso to prove the inspired writings folly and fable—impossible, incredible, absurd,—and we scarcely remember what other names he has used, to show how his mind soars above the assumed wisdom and truth of the sacred writings.

The next principle of cavilling, to carry out this vicious system of reasoning which the Bishop of Natal adopts, is, by the consent of all honest and enlightened minds, the lowest, and the most to be despised. We allude to the principle of seeking to involve a man in falsehood by a petty system of cavils and contradictions extracted from his own words.

This is not to follow the path of truth. It is the mode adopted by some ignorant and bullying lawyers, in order to " browbeat" a witness. But it is a way as far removed from all dignity of mind as light is from darkness; and, though it take with the multitude,—" at saltem hoc tenet nos,"—as Horace said of the brawler for " civil and religious liberty " of his day, whose voice could drown the noise of several waggons and funerals; or, like Goldsmith's village-schoolmaster, whose

" Words of learned length, and thundering sound,
Amazed the gazing rustics ranged around,
And still they gazed, and still the wonder grew,
That one small head could carry all he knew;"—

but though, we say, all this may take with many, and especially with infidels, who catch at any thing that can insult their Maker, and their Maker's Word, yet it is as short-lived as the inflated bubbles forced up on the surface of the stream.

This, then, is the other mode of argument adopted by Bishop Colenso to sap the foundation of Faith. We shall only say, that if the authors of such a wretched system of arguing, and of such insults to the sacred writers, were to be matched against, and for only five minutes within the grasp of a man of such mind as Moses possessed, there would be such an exhibition made of them, and of their learned sophistry, as would for ever silence their tongues, even though it should not cure their vanity.

If Bishop Colenso desire to destroy all belief in the Word of God, he should, in place of such a system of objections and cavils, bring forward positive evidence which, by its weight, would overthrow the evidence by which the writings of Moses, as a prominent part of the revelation of God, have been in all ages, and are to this day, sustained.

But, until the Bishop of Natal can do this, all believers in the Word of God may rest in peace. And in order to draw, as he seeks to do, the multitude after him, Bishop Colenso should prove, or pretend, a call from heaven, and a new revelation to man. But he must not expect to argue men out of their common sense by such cavils and sophistry as those which his book displays. If the Almighty has established His Revelation by such infallible signs, and wonders, and standing monuments, and testimony that grows with age, and shows not any appearance of decay, then it is indeed of very little consequence that any man should say that the Almighty could not have spoken to His creatures, or that He must have spoken only in the way which Bishop Colenso would allow.

And now if we were to become converts to the principles of Bishop Colenso, and reject the writings of Moses as fable and falsehood, and with them the whole Revelation of God; for, as we have showed, even the mission and words of Christ Himself, by His own declaration, must stand or fall with the "fable" of Moses;—what, we may very naturally ask, does Bishop Colenso propose to give us in the place of Christianity, which he would overthrow? This is the question.

We recommend to the Bishop of Natal, and to modern reformers of the Bible, the following passage from the pen of the well-known wit and political divine of the reign of Queen Anne:—

"INCONVENIENCES FROM A PROPOSED ABOLITION OF CHRISTIANITY.

"I am very sensible how much the gentlemen of

wit and pleasure are apt to murmur, and be shocked at the sight of so many daggle-tail parsons who happen to fall in their way, and offend their eyes; but, at the same time, those wise reformers do not consider what an advantage and felicity it is for great wits to be always provided with objects of scorn and contempt in order to exercise and improve their talents, and divert their spleen from falling on each other, or on themselves; especially when all this may be done without the least imaginable danger to their persons. And, to urge another argument of a parallel nature:—If Christianity were once abolished, how could the freethinkers, the strong reasoners, and the men of profound learning, be able to find another subject so calculated in all points whereon to display their abilities? What wonderful productions of wit should we be deprived of from those whose genius by continual practice hath been wholly turned upon raillery and invectives against religion, and would therefore be never able to shine or distinguish themselves on any other subject? We are daily complaining of the great decline of wit among us; and would we take away the greatest, perhaps the only topic we have left? Who would ever have suspected Asgill for a wit, or Toland for a philosopher, if the inexhaustible stock of Christianity had not been at hand to provide them with materials? What other subject through all art or nature could have produced Tindal for a profound author, or furnished him with readers? It is the wise choice of the subject that alone adorneth and distinguisheth the writer: for, had a hundred such pens as these been employed on the side of religion, they would immediately have sunk into silence and oblivion."

Our author then states another "inconvenience"

which might arise from the "abolition of Christianity," viz. that the Church would be in danger! And this "inconvenience" would be attended with such serious results, more especially, we may add, to those who eat the bread of the Church and lift up their heel against it, and against the Revelation of the Church's Lord;— that these, and, above all, as our author says, the danger that "Presbytery might come in," are "considerations to be left to the men in power!"

What, then, does the Bishop of Natal propose to give us in the place of Christianity?—for we repeat again and again, this is the question—the only real question at issue.

It is idle to speak of the Christian religion as containing noble sentiments and useful precepts. Even the well-known infidel of the great French revolution could rebuke his friend for daring to make any comparison between Socrates and Christ; and after allowing Socrates all due credit, could yet ask, "But where could Jesus have learned amongst his competitors that pure and sublime morality of which He only has given us both precept and example?"

But pure and sublime morality is not Christianity. The light of nature, or Natural Religion, has given, and can give, most noble sentiments. But though Christ spake as "never man spake," yet Christianity is not a mere republication of Natural Religion in an improved edition.

Christianity is the revelation, begun in the writings of Moses and perfected in the Gospel, of a plan of mercy and salvation for the recovery of fallen man;—a plan which the light of nature, or Natural Religion, never taught, and never can teach, to the lost and wandering race of Adam. The poet well wrote, who thus described our lot in this life:—

> "Poor wanderers of a stormy day!
> From wave to wave we're driven,
> And fancy's flash, and reason's ray,
> Serve but to light the troubled way:
> There's nothing calm but Heaven."

It is idle, therefore, to speak of leaving men some portion of the Bible, such as our modern sages would select, or to leave us the mere precepts of the Gospel.

If the Bishop of Natal were to succeed in his effort to overthrow the Revelation of God,—although, poor man! he might as well try, by his figures and calculations, to pull down the noon-day sun from the firmament of the heavens,—yet, for the sake of argument, we say, if he were to succeed to the utmost extent of his efforts, what does he propose to give us in return for the Revelation of God, which he would consign to contempt and oblivion?

Should any reply,—The light of nature, or Natural Religion; we answer,— Most certainly not. The Bishop, it is true, quotes sentiments of men who acted and wrote under the light of nature, or, as taught by uncorrupted Natural Religion. But the light of nature, or Natural Religion, is not that which Bishop Colenso would substitute in the place of the Word of God. We deny this altogether.

The light of nature is from God, and can, as it does, teach the noblest sentiments; but it cannot teach the way of salvation; it cannot "guide our feet into the way of peace." St. Paul shows, what reason confirms, that men are condemned by the light of nature, not for rejection of the Gospel if not preached to them, but for idolatry,— because they could know enough of God from His works to leave idolatry without excuse.

And, in the days of Job, the idolatry which consisted

in the worship of even the works of God's hands, such as the sun and moon, was an offence to be "punished by the judge," on the ground of its denying "the God that is above." St. Paul also shows that of which Moses gave warning, that if men were to worship even the works of God,—God, so justly insulted, would give them up, as St. Paul shows the heathen world was given up, to descend in the scale of idolatry, and worship the works of their own hands and of their own corrupt minds. And then they were to be further given up to reprobate minds, " to work all uncleanness with greediness;" and to bring forth all those fruits which are the shame and disgrace of the human family.

All such peculiar debasement arose from corruption of the light of nature, or of Natural Religion. And all the gods under this corruption of Natural Religion were the personification and deification of all the depravity of which fallen man is, has been, or ever can be capable.

But the wisest and best of the heathen philosophers soared far above the worship of those debased and debasing deities. They worshipped the God of Nature, the Creator of the Universe, and to the utmost of their ability followed the only light which they received from God.

But not such the religion which the book of Bishop Colenso would propagate. His work would establish another "Age of Reason;" an accursed, brutal, and brutalizing creed. This character of such a system is what reason would pronounce, and what experience will confirm. We repeat, accursed creed; for there is not any curse that can desolate earth to a greater extent, or convert the world into a den of felons, more effectually than the principles of the "Age of Reason." This is the righteous law of Providence. The most terrible instruments for promotion of misery on earth are the best blessings of God when perverted by man; and, as reason is the noblest gift of the Creator, so perverted reason is the most terrible curse.

We judge of the book of Bishop Colenso for ourselves, and apart from all questions which agitate and divide the Church. And we are constrained to say that we never read, or reviewed, a book which displayed more bitter, though feeble, malignity against the Revelation of God.

In answer to the wonder that Bishop Colenso,—who has not, like Moses, filled the world with his fame,—should be so foolish as to send forth his nerveless attack on the work of such a master-mind, the apologists of the Bishop reply, that the Bishop does not admit that Moses was the writer of the Pentateuch.

The answer is ready. Then the Lord Jesus Christ sent forth a falsehood! This is one result of this "Age of Reason!"

It is, then, infidelity,—and infidelity based on the overthrow of the sacred writers, on the very ruins of Christianity,—which Bishop Colenso's book would propagate. And that infidelity we cannot better describe than in the words of Burke, "That foul and unnatural vice, foe to all the dignity and consolation of mankind."

Infidelity is a vice, and one of the most destructive vices, of the mind; and one which, unlike the vices of the body, does not afford any kind of pleasure, for the slave to vice of the body does find some gratification;—but this vice of infidelity does not, cannot, afford any, save the fiendish satisfaction of smiling with complacency at the ruin which it makes.

And what would be the effects of this infidelity, of this "Age of Reason," if not restrained by the influence of that Revelation which those men of reason would overthrow? Let us hear the voice of nature in the grand language of our immortal Shakespeare, and, from his sublime description, we may form some idea of the state of things if the light of heaven were to be withdrawn; as well as of the way in which that light controls, and puts to shame those deeds of darkness which would otherwise overrun and destroy the land.

> " Discomfortable cousin! know'st thou not,
> That when the searching eye of heaven is hid
> Behind the globe, and lights the lower world,
> Then thieves and robbers range abroad unseen,
> In murders and in outrage bloody here;
> But when, from under this terrestrial ball,
> He fires the proud tops of the eastern pines,
> And darts his light through every guilty hole,
> Then murders, treasons, and detested sins,
> The cloak of night being pluck'd from off their backs,
> Stand bare and naked, trembling at themselves?"

"By their fruits ye shall know them," said Truth itself.

The first professor of this religion of reason was Cain. He did not consider, that reason was not bestowed on man that it might set up itself against the wisdom of the Creator, but to receive His word, however or wherever spoken to His creatures. But Cain thought the doctrine of sacrifice a very foolish thing. "How can the slaying of a lamb place me in a state of favour with God? Besides, I cannot see how such a thing should be necessary; I am good enough for the society of even God Himself."

With such reasonings Cain darkened "counsel, by words without knowledge;" and he refused to believe, and act upon, the promise of the Lamb of God that was to be slain, in due time, to take away the sin of the world. "If I am a sinner, God can forgive me without any sacrifice. I am quite ready to make an offering to the Creator of the fruits of the ground; for the least portion of common sense tells me that those fruits could not create themselves. But beyond this I will not go. I am not to be expected to cramp my reasoning powers, or to be tied down to any foolish opinions."

Abel was of a very different mind; but then Abel was not a philosopher of the school of reason; but one who received, with childlike submission, the Revelation of his Maker. And Abel sacrificed "of the firstlings of his flock;" "and the Lord had respect unto Abel and to his offering" was the response; and, after the lapse of four thousand years, the Apostle wrote, "and by it he being dead yet speaketh." "But unto Cain and his offering He had not respect."

But all this was, perhaps, after all, merely a speculative opinion, an exercise of reason, and why should the mind of Cain have been chained down to any dogma? And, besides, it would have been very improper to have put any curb on "the spirit of free inquiry," or to have interfered with "tender consciences." But was this first instance of acting on the principles of "the age of reason," such a harmless doctrine, the mere exercise of the spirit of inquiry, or of a tender conscience?

What were the fruits of this free inquiry? Cain first was wroth, for he envied his brother, and, at last, "Cain rose up against Abel his brother, and slew him." And when asked a simple question, "Where is Abel thy brother?" he answered, "I know not," and then sent forth the doctrine, "Am I my brother's keeper?" This doctrine of the age of reason has deluged the earth with crime and misery. This doctrine keeps man from man, and breaks the social tie; and it makes man a solitary individual in the midst of millions of his fellow-creatures.

Now we will not insult the Holy Scriptures by contrasting their sentiments and precepts with such doctrine as this; doctrine, the natural consequence of the religion of the age of reason. We propose to draw our contrast from the religion of the light of nature, and, though we might fill chapters with selections from heathen authors of the noble sentiments, and acts, of men who had for their guides only the light of nature, and conscience, "the deputy of God in man," we shall confine ourselves to one instance, as it affords a striking contrast with the doctrine and practice of Cain.

When Cæsar reached the gates of Utica, and found that Cato had destroyed himself, rather than fall into the hands of his enemy, the great conqueror is reported to have exclaimed, "Cato has robbed me of my noblest victory, for I meant to have pardoned him all the wrongs that he had done me." This was the religion of the light of nature, of which God is the Author, but the act and doctrine of Cain were the result of following the religion of the "age of reason;" of which the "devil," who was "a liar and a murderer from the beginning," is the father and the founder.

It was the same religion, that of the light of nature, not corrupted by the perverted reason of man, that gave rise to the grand sentiments of heathen philosophers quoted in some of our preceding chapters. We now bring forward this speech of Cæsar, merely because it bears upon the subject under review, and, as a mere illustration of our argument; and we shall now conclude with a still more practical view of the question.

The pages of history present an instance, in which the disciples of the age of reason obtained the supreme power in a mighty empire. What was the result? A dignitary of the Church, an archbishop, was found to come forward, and, on behalf of the nation, renounce the "fable" of Moses, and the sacred writings with which that "fable" is inseparably connected. But it is only an act of justice to say, that the largest body of the clergy of that kingdom refused to follow their degenerate leader, and they submitted to unheard-of trials and cruel deaths.

The next step in this "unchaining of the human mind," this establishing of "free inquiry" was, that a wretched being styled "the Goddess of Reason" was crowned, and placed on an ass, and the Bible was dragged at the tail of the ass through the public streets. And then the most horrible "hell-hounds of savage war" were let loose upon the doomed people of that unhappy country.

Language would fail to describe the fruits of the curse which fell on the degraded and devoted nation. Let us hear two witnesses on this subject: the first, our great political philosopher; the second, an eminent American divine. Let us, then, first hear the testimony of Edmund Burke.

"In a political view, France was low indeed; she had lost every thing, even to her name:—

'—— jacet ingens littore truncus,
Avolsumque humeris caput et sine nomine corpus.'

He was astonished at it; he was alarmed at it; he trembled at the uncertainty of all human greatness. Since the house had been prorogued in summer much work had been done in France. The French had shown themselves the noblest architects of ruin that had hitherto existed in the world. In that short space of time they had completely pulled down to the ground their monarchy; their church; their nobility; their law; their revenue; their army; their navy; their commerce; their arts; and their manufacture. They had done their business for us as rivals in a way in which twenty Ramillies or Blenheims could never have done it. Were we absolute conquerors, and France to lie prostrate at our feet, we should be ashamed to send a commission to settle their affairs, which could impose as hard a law upon the French, and so destructive of all their consequence as a nation, as that which they had imposed upon themselves."

Let us now hear the testimony of Dwight:—"The only instance in which infidels of any description have possessed the supreme power and government of a country, and have attempted to dispose of human happiness according to their own doctrines and wishes, is that of *France*, since the beginning of the Revolution. If we consider this government as established over a nation educated for ages to the belief and obedience of many doctrines of Christianity, and retaining, as to a great majority of the people, the habits formed by that education, the state of that nation will evince, beyond a question, that all which I have said is true without exaggeration.

"*France*, during this period, has been a theatre of crimes, which, after all preceding perpetrations, have excited in the mind of every spectator amazement and horror. The miseries suffered by that single nation have changed all the histories of the preceding sufferings of mankind into idle tales, and have been enhanced, and multiplied without a precedent, without number, and without a name. The kingdom appeared to be changed into one great prison; the inhabitants converted into felons; and the common doom of man commuted for the violence of the sword and the bayonet, the sucking-boat and the guillotine.

"To contemplative men it seemed for a season, as if the knell of the whole nation was tolled, and the world summoned to its execution and its funeral. Within the short time of ten years, not less than three millions of human beings are supposed to have perished, in that single country, by the influence of Atheism. Were the world to adopt and be governed by the doctrines of *France*, what crimes would not mankind perpetrate; what agonies would they not suffer?"

In the eloquent and vigorous words of those two great men, we have a just description of the horrors which followed, and must ever follow, contempt of God's Holy Word, and of the establishment of "The Age of Reason." "Do men gather grapes of thorns or figs of thistles?" Probably some of the very actors in those dreadful scenes would have repelled, with indignation, the idea that themselves, or their principles, could have brought about such results. "Is thy servant a dog that he should do this thing?" may be ready on the tongue. But when men once send forth principles which contain but the mere seeds of infidelity, they must not wonder, if a full harvest of destruction should in due time arrive. And when once the evil spirit is let loose, it is not in the power of man to beguile that spirit into its prison-house again.

"Let us now," in the language of the same eloquent writer, Dr. Dwight, "turn our view from this prospect of guilt and desolation, this dark and final abyss of sin and ruin, where no solitary virtue gleams, where no ray of hope or comfort trembles through profound midnight, and refresh the wearied sight by casting a momentary glance over the moral world of the Christian. Here, at the head of the vast chain of moral being, reaching like *Jacob's* ladder from earth to heaven, sits on the throne of infinite dominion the God of *Abraham*, the God of *Isaac*, the God of *Jacob*, the God of all, who, like them, believe, worship, and obey their Creator. In Him the Self-existent and Infinite Mind, the Christian beholds unceasingly an object of boundless sublimity, grandeur, beauty, and loveliness: commanding by the disclosure of His character, and exhausting all finite admiration, complacency, love, and praise; expanding every view, refining every affection, and ennobling every attribute.

"From the immediate contemplation of this glorious Being, raised to a superiority and distinction, of which he could otherwise have never conceived, he casts his eyes abroad into the Universe which That Being has created. There he beholds an endless train of intelligent minds, reflecting with no unhappy lustre, the beauty and glory of their Maker. From the pre-eminent dignity of the Archangel, through the glowing zeal of the Seraph, and the milder wisdom of the Cherub; through the high endowments of *Moses, Isaiah,* and *Paul,* down to the humble but virtuous inhabitant of a cottage, one spirit lives, and breathes, and actuates in all; and that spirit is divine. Each wears, and exhibits, in his own manner, and that manner a delightful and useful one, the image and beauty of JEHOVAH.

"All, though of different magnitudes, diffuse a real light; all are stars, though *one star differeth from another star in glory.* All are the subjects of virtuous affections: all are fitted to admire and adore, to glorify and enjoy, their Creator; all are formed, and disposed voluntarily, to fill up their existence with doing good, with promoting individual enjoyment, and increasing universal happiness: all are bound together as children of one God, and brethren of each other, by *love, the bond of perfection.* Every one, therefore, is lovely in the sight of his Maker.

"To this universe of minds the Christian believes that the Creator, who is, of course, the rightful lawgiver, has given laws for the direction of its members which require perfect conduct and ensure to it perfect happiness. These laws extend to all the thoughts, words, and actions, alike; and regulate each with unerring propriety. Their obligation is, and is acknowledged to be, divine; nothing can sunder, nothing can lessen it. This, instead of being a source of regret to him, is his delight; for what these laws require is better than any thing else, and more fraught with self-approbation, worth, and enjoyment.

"Of course, in all the relations and situations in life, as a parent, or a child, a neighbour, or a friend, a magistrate, or a subject, he feels himself on the one hand irresistibly obliged, and on the other entirely delighted to obey their dictates. As these dictates reach every moral being in every situation, and with respect to every action, they provide of course, and universally, for that conduct in every being, which is commendable and desirable.

"Here an immoveable foundation is laid for peace within, for dignity of mind, for real and enduring enjoyment in the recesses of solitude, and for the endless train of duties and blessings necessary to the happiness of society. A ruler formed in this manner will govern only to bless; subjects of the same character will obey because rectitude demands their obedience, and because their obedience will ensure the happiness both of themselves and their rulers."

In the passages now quoted from those two distinguished men, you have, reader, a true picture of scenes which would again follow the subjugation of the Record of Mercy to the shallow wisdom of man; and the consequent establishment of the principles of an "Age of Reason." The tendency of the work of Bishop Colenso is to promote such dangerous and destructive principles. It is of little consequence to any who desire the happiness of themselves and of society, whether Bishop Colenso intend such a result, or whether he see the nature of his efforts to throw discredit and contempt on the compilers of the Holy Scriptures. And it would be an insult to common sense to discuss the question as to the Bishop and his school being amiable, or sincere, or well-meaning, or conscientious, or any such-like unmeaning terms, which we so constantly hear; as if the personal qualities of any individual were the standard of faith and morality. What have we to do with such questions? Is the well-being of society to be suspended on the personal feelings, or qualifications, of any of those modern thinkers who set themselves up to condemn, reject, alter, and amend at pleasure the Revelation of God? We have to do only with the principles which those men would establish in the place of the sacred writings,—principles with which those revilers of Moses would deluge society, and sweep away all true religion, and all happiness and peace, from the land. Judge, then, reader, for yourself; and behold the nature and the effects of that truly cursed system of perverted reason which a Christian Bishop would substitute for the "fable" of Moses, and the Revelation of God, under the shadow of which England arose from a state of moral death, and grew until she became the wonder and the envy of the nations of the earth. Yes; under the light and influence of that Revelation of God, England became what she is, and what we pray that she may long continue—"a great and free monarchy, which knows how to be great without endangering its own peace at home, or the internal or external peace of any of its neighbours." But in the days of old, England was very different from what this picture paints to the eye. Cicero, Cæsar, and Virgil—all describe the Britain of their day as the habitation of barbarism and debasement.

It was not a system of arithmetic that made England the commandingly-beautiful object — even with her many faults — which she now presents to the mind — the glory of all lands.

It is, therefore, contrary to nature to have an Englishman seek to reason any man into contempt of God's Holy Word, and into belief of comfortless and blighting infidelity. What Burke said on the subject of our bad government of America, will well apply in this place:—" We cannot, I fear, falsify the pedigree of this fierce people, and persuade them that they are not sprung from a nation in whose veins the blood of freedom circulates. The language in which they would hear you tell them this tale would detect the imposition. Your speech would betray you. An Englishman is the unfittest person on earth to argue another Englishman into slavery."

And if so unnatural for an Englishman to seek to argue another Englishman into slavery, how much more unnatural for any Englishman — and O shame! for a Christian Bishop, — to seek to argue any Englishman into infidelity? Therefore, reader, stand by the old landmarks of truth and freedom, and be not brought into bondage under this "Age of Reason." When now called on to choose between the Revelation of God, and the "Age of Reason," act on the determination of the good king, — and, in his choice, true philosopher!—" Let us now fall into the hand of the Lord; for His mercies are great: and let me not fall into the hand of man." And learn to prize more than ever the beauty and truth of that prayer of our Church, which ascends to Almighty God every Sabbath from pulpits almost beyond number, in every part of the earth where our language has found an entrance:—

" BLESSED LORD, who hast caused all Holy Scriptures to be written for our learning; grant that we may in such wise hear them, read, mark, learn, and inwardly digest them; that by patience and comfort of Thy Holy Word, we may embrace, and ever hold fast the blessed hope of everlasting life, which Thou hast given us in our SAVIOUR JESUS CHRIST. Amen."

THE END.

February, 1863.

NEW WORKS AND NEW EDITIONS,

PUBLISHED BY

MESSRS. RIVINGTON,

3, WATERLOO PLACE, PALL MALL, LONDON.

McCaul.—An Examination of Bishop Colenso's Difficulties with regard to the Pentateuch. By the Rev. Alexander McCaul, D.D., Professor of Hebrew and Old Testament Exegesis, King's College, London. Crown 8vo. (*In the press.*)

Wordsworth.—Journal of a Tour in Italy; particularly with reference to the Present Condition and Prospects of Religion in that country. By Chr. Wordsworth, D.D., Canon of Westminster. In Two Vols., post 8vo. 15s. (*Now ready.*)

Alford.—The New Testament for English Readers: consisting of the Authorized Version of the Sacred Text; Marginal References; Various Readings; and a Popular Commentary. By Henry Alford, D.D., Dean of Canterbury. In Two Volumes, 8vo. (*In the press.*)

Clissold.—Lamps of the Church; or, Rays of Faith, Hope, and Charity, from the Lives and Deaths of some Eminent Christians of the Nineteenth Century. By the Rev. H. Clissold, M.A., Author of I. "Last Hours of Eminent Christian Men;" II. "Last Hours of Eminent Christian Women." Crown 8vo., *with five Portraits beautifully engraved on Steel.* 9s. 6d. (*Now ready.*)

⁎ In this volume will be found Memorials of William Cowper—Henry Kirke White—Henry Martyn—Claudius Buchanan—John Bowdler—Thomas Rennell—Legh Richmond—Hannah More—Mary Jane Graham—William Wilberforce—Thomas Arnold—Robert Anderson—Hedley Vicars—Bishop Armstrong—Bishop Blomfield—and many others.

Moreton.—Life and Work in Newfoundland: Reminiscences of Thirteen Years spent there. By the Rev. Julian Moreton, Colonial Chaplain at Labuan. Crown 8vo., *with Illustrations*. (*In the press.*)

Boyle.—The Inspiration of the Book of Daniel, and incidentally of other portions of Sacred Scripture. With a correction of Profane, and an adjustment of Sacred Chronology. By W. R. A. Boyle. 8vo. (*In the press.*)

Goulburn.—Lectures on the English Office of the Holy Communion. By Edward Meyrick Goulburn, D.D., Prebendary of St. Paul's, and one of Her Majesty's Chaplains in Ordinary. In Two Vols., small 8vo. (*In the press*).

Seymour. Mackarness.—Eighteen Years of a Clerical Meeting: being the Minutes of the Alcester Clerical Association, from 1842 to 1860; with a Preface on the Revival of Ruridecanal Chapters. Edited by Richard Seymour, M.A., Rector of Kinwarton and Rural Dean; and John F. Mackarness, M.A., late Vicar of Tardebigge, in the Diocese of Worcester, now Rector of Honiton. Crown 8vo. 6s. 6d.

Mackenzie.—Ordination Lectures, delivered in Riseholme Palace Chapel, during Ember Weeks. By the Rev. Henry Mackenzie, M.A., one of the Chaplains to the Lord Bishop of Lincoln, &c. &c. Small 8vo. 3s.

CONTENTS:—Pastoral Government—Educational Work—Self-government in the Pastor—Missions and their Reflex Results—Dissent—Public Teaching—Sunday Schools—Doctrinal Controversy—Secular Aids.

Alford.—Sermons on Christian Doctrine, preached in Canterbury Cathedral, on the Afternoons of the Sundays in the year 1861-62. By Henry Alford, D.D., Dean of Canterbury. In crown 8vo. 7s. 6d. (*Lately published.*)

RIVINGTONS, WATERLOO PLACE, LONDON.

NEW WORKS AND NEW EDITIONS.

McCaul.—Testimonies to the Divine Authority and Inspiration of Holy Scripture, as taught by the Church of England. By the Rev. A. McCaul, D.D., Prebendary of St. Paul's, Professor of Ecclesiastical History at King's College, and Rector of St. Magnus. Crown 8vo. 4s. 6d. (*Lately published.*)

Gurney.—Sermons on the Acts of the Apostles. By John Hampden Gurney, M.A., late Rector of St. Mary's Church, Marylebone. Small 8vo. 7s. (*Just published.*)

Lately published by the same Author,

Sermons chiefly on Old Testament Histories, from Texts in the Sunday Lessons. *Second Edition.* 6s.

Sermons on Texts from the Epistles and Gospels for twenty Sundays. *Second Edition.* 6s.

Miscellaneous Sermons. 6s.

Goulburn.—Thoughts on Personal Religion. By Edward Meyrick Goulburn, D.D., Prebendary of St. Paul's, and one of Her Majesty's Chaplains in Ordinary. *Third Edition*, with two additional Chapters. Small 8vo. 6s. 6d.

Williams.—The Beginning of the Book of Genesis, with Notes and Reflections. By the Rev. Isaac Williams, B.D. Printed uniformly with Mr. Williams's Harmony and Commentary on the Gospels, in small 8vo. 7s. 6d.

Greswell.—The Three Witnesses, and the Threefold Cord; being the testimony of the Natural Measures of Time, of the Primitive Civil Calendar, and of Antediluvian and Postdiluvian Tradition, on the principal questions of fact in sacred or profane Antiquity. By Edward Greswell, B.D., Fellow of Corpus Christi College, Oxford. 8vo. 7s. 6d. (*Lately published.*)

Mozley.—A Review of the Baptismal Controversy. By J. B. Mozley, B.D., Vicar of Old Shoreham, late Fellow of Magdalen College, Oxford. 8vo. 9s. 6d. (*Lately published.*)

RIVINGTONS, WATERLOO PLACE, LONDON.

Williams.—A Devotional Commentary on the Book of Psalms. By the Rev. Isaac Williams, B.D., late Fellow of Trinity College, Oxford. In Three Vols., small 8vo. (*In the press.*)

Clabon.—Praise, Precept, and Prayer; a Complete Manual of Family Worship. By J. M. Clabon. In One large Volume, 8vo. 16s.

Markby.—The Man Christ Jesus; or, the Daily Life, and Teaching of our Lord, in Childhood and Manhood, on Earth. By the Rev. Thomas Markby, M.A., lately Afternoon Lecturer at St. James's, Paddington. Crown 8vo. 9s. 6d.

Notes on Wild Flowers.—By a Lady. Small 8vo. (*In the press.*)

Goulburn.—Sermons preached on Various Occasions during the last Twenty Years. By Edward Meyrick Goulburn, D.D. In Two Vols., small 8vo. 10s. 6d.

Devotional.—The Threshold of Private Devotion; containing Prayers, and Extracts from the Holy Scriptures and from Various Authors. 18mo. 2s.

Williams.—Female Characters of Holy Scripture; in a Series of Sermons. By the Rev. Isaac Williams, B.D., late Fellow of Trinity College, Oxford. *Second Edition.* Small 8vo. 5s. 6d.

Wordsworth.—The Holy Year; Hymns for Sundays and Holydays, and for other Occasions. By Chr. Wordsworth, D.D., Canon of Westminster. Small 8vo. 4s. 6d. in extra cloth, or 10s. 6d. in morocco. Also a cheaper Edition, price 2s. 6d.

Page.—The Pretensions of Bishop Colenso to impeach the Wisdom and Veracity of the Compilers of the Holy Scriptures considered. By the Rev. James R. Page, M.A., Editor of "Burnet's Exposition of the Thirty-nine Articles;" Author of "Position of the Church of England in the Catholic World," and other works. 8vo. (*In the press.*)

RIVINGTONS, WATERLOO PLACE, LONDON.

Alford.—The Greek Testament; with a critically revised Text: a Digest of Various Readings: Marginal References to Verbal and Idiomatic Usage: Prolegomena: and a copious Critical and Exegetical Commentary in English. For the Use of Theological Students and Ministers. By Henry Alford, D.D., Dean of Canterbury. In Four Vols., 8vo.

    Vol. I.—The Four Gospels. *A Fifth Edition is in the press.*
    Vol. II.—Acts to II. Corinthians. *Fourth Edition.* 24s.
    Vol. III.—Galatians to Philemon. *Third Edition.* 18s.
    Vol. IV.—Hebrews to Revelation. *Second Edition.* 32s.
    The fourth Volume may still be had in Two Parts.

Knowles.—Notes on the Epistle to the Hebrews, with Analysis and Brief Paraphrase; for Theological Students. Dedicated by permission to the Lord Bishop of Oxford. By the Rev. E. H. Knowles, late Michel Fellow of Queen's College, Oxford. Crown 8vo. 6s. 6d.

The Annual Register; or, a View of the History and Politics of the Year 1861. 8vo. 18s.

Peile.—The Miracle of Healing Power. Christ in His Man's Nature through Death Man's Quickener into Life in God: an Argument from Scripture only. By Thomas Williamson Peile, D.D., Incumbent of St. Paul's, Hampstead, late Vicar of Luton, Beds, and sometime Fellow of Trinity College, Cambridge. 8vo. 5s.

Crosthwaite.—Eight Lectures on the Historical Events and Characters in the Book of Daniel: to which are added, Four Discourses on the Doctrine of our Mutual Recognition in a Future State. Inscribed, by permission, to his Grace the late Archbishop of Armagh. By the Rev. J. C. Crosthwaite, M.A., Rector of St. Mary-at-Hill, London. 12mo. (*In the press.*)

Adams.—The Shadow of the Cross: an Allegory. By the late Rev. W. Adams, M.A. A New Edition, elegantly printed in crown 8vo., with Illustrations, price 3s. 6d. in extra cloth, gilt edges.

Douglas.—Sermons. By Henry Alexander Douglas, M.A., Dean of Cape Town. 12mo. 4s. 6d.

Green.—Brief Memorials of the late Rev. Charles Green, M.A., of Worcester College, Oxford; Missionary and Secretary of the Society for the Propagation of the Gospel. Small 8vo. 2s. 6d.

Wordsworth.—The New Testament of our Lord and Saviour Jesus Christ, in the Original Greek. With Notes, Introductions, and Indexes. By Chr. Wordsworth, D.D., Canon of Westminster. *New Edition.* In Two Vols., imperial 8vo. 4*l.*

Or separately,

Part I.: The Four Gospels. *New Edition.* 1*l.* 1s.
Part II.: The Acts. *New Edition.* 10s. 6d.
Part III.: The Epistles of St. Paul. *New Edition.* 1*l.* 11s. 6d.
Part IV.: The General Epistles and Book of Revelation; with Indexes. *New Edition.* 1*l.* 1s.

Goulburn.—An Introduction to the Devotional Study of the Holy Scriptures. By Edward Meyrick Goulburn, D.D. *Fifth Edition.* Small 8vo. 4s. 6d.

Roman Biography. — De Viris Illustribus Urbis Romæ, a Romulo ad Augustum. An Elementary Latin Reading Book, being a Series of Biographical Chapters on Roman History, chronologically arranged; simplified from the Text of Livy and other Roman writers; adapted, with Annotations and a Vocabulary, from the work of Professor Lhomond. By the Editor of the "Graduated Series of English Reading Books." Small 8vo. 3s.

Atkins.—Six Discourses on Pastoral Duties, preached before the University of Dublin; being the Donnellan Lectures for 1860. By William Atkins, D.D., formerly Fellow of Trinity College, Dublin; Rector of Tullyagnish, Diocese of Raphoe; and Examining Chaplain to the Lord Bishop of Derry. 8vo. 6s.

Alford.—Reminiscences by a Clergyman's Wife. Edited by The Dean of Canterbury. *Second Edition.* Crown 8vo. 3s. 6d.

Glover.—England, the Remnant of Judah, and the Israel of Ephraim. By the Rev. F. R. A. Glover, M.A., Chaplain to the Consulate at Cologne. 8vo. 6s. 6d.

Miller.—Parochial Sermons. By the Rev. J. K. Miller, late Vicar of Walkeringham, Notts, and formerly Fellow of Trinity College, Cambridge. Small 8vo. 4s. 6d.

Hawkins.—The Limits of Religious Belief: Suggestions addressed to the Student in Divine Things. By the Rev. Wm. Bentinck Hawkins, M.A., F.R.S., of Exeter College, Oxford. Small 8vo. 2s. 6d.

Wordsworth.—The Inspiration of the Bible; Five Lectures, delivered in Westminster Abbey. By Christopher Wordsworth, D.D., Canon of Westminster. Post 8vo. 3s. 6d.

Wordsworth.—The Interpretation of the Bible; Five Lectures, delivered in Westminster Abbey. By the same Author. Post 8vo. 3s. 6d.

Galloway.—Ezekiel's Sign, Metrically Paraphrased and Interpreted, from his Fourth and Fifth Chapters; with Notes and Elucidations from the Sculptured Slabs of Nineveh. By W. B. Galloway, M.A., Incumbent of St. Mark's, Regent's Park, and Chaplain to the Viscount Hawarden. Small 8vo. 2s. 6d.

Byng.—Sermons for Households. By Francis E. C. Byng, M.A., Rector of Little Casterton. Crown 8vo. 3s. 6d.

Henley.—The Prayer of Prayers. By the Hon. and Rev. Robert Henley, M.A., Perpetual Curate of Putney. Small 8vo. 4s. 6d.

RIVINGTONS, WATERLOO PLACE, LONDON.

Warter.—The Sea-board and the Down; or, My Parish in the South. By John Wood Warter, B.D., Vicar of West Tarring, Sussex. In Two Vols., small 4to., with Illustrations. 28s.

Trevelyan.—Quarr Abbey, or the Mistaken Calling; a Tale of the Isle of Wight in the Thirteenth Century. By Frances A. Trevelyan, Author of "Lectures on English History." Small 4to., price 1s. 6d., or in cloth, with Illustrations, 2s. 6d.

Monsell.—Parish Musings; or, Devotional Poems. By John S. B. Monsell, LL.D., Vicar of Egham, Surrey, and Rural Dean. *Fifth Edition.* 2s.

Hooper.—The Revelation of Jesus Christ; expounded by Francis Bodfield Hooper, Rector of Upton Warren, Worcestershire, Author of "A Guide to the Apocalypse," and other Works. In Two Vols., 8vo. 28s.

Hodgson.—Instructions for the Use of Candidates for Holy Orders, and of the Parochial Clergy, as to Ordination, Licences, Induction, Pluralities, Residence, &c. &c., with Acts of Parliament relating to the above, and Forms to be used. By Christopher Hodgson, M.A., Secretary to the Governors of Queen Anne's Bounty. *Eighth Edition.* In 8vo. 12s.

⁎ In this Edition such alterations have been made as appeared to be necessary in consequence of recent amendments in the laws relating to the Clergy.

Giles.—Village Sermons, preached at some of the chief Christian Seasons, in the Parish Church of Belleau with Aby. By J. D. Giles, M.A., late Rector. Small 8vo. 5s.

RIVINGTONS, WATERLOO PLACE, LONDON.

PAMPHLETS LATELY PUBLISHED

BY

MESSRS. RIVINGTON.

A Letter to the Clergy of the Diocese of Llandaff, in reference to the Critical Examination of the Pentateuch by the Bishop of Natal. By Alfred Ollivant, D.D., Bishop of Llandaff. 8vo. 1s. 6d.

Plain Possible Solutions of the Objections of the Right Rev. John William Colenso, D.D., Bishop of Natal. By the Rev. George Vallis Garland, M.A., Rector of Langton Matravers, Dorset. 8vo. 1s. 6d.

An Answer to the Difficulties in Bishop Colenso's Book on the Pentateuch. By the Rev. J. B. Turner, Vicar of Marsworth, Bucks. 8vo. 1s.

Letter to Bishop Colenso, wherein his Objections to the Pentateuch are Examined in Detail. By the Rev. William H. Hoare, M.A. *Second Edition.* 8vo. 1s.

Parochial Mission-Women; their Work and its Fruits. By the Hon. Mrs. J. C. Talbot. *Second Edition.* Small 8vo. 2s. in limp cloth.

Five Short Letters to Sir William Heathcote, Bart., M.P. for the University of Oxford, on the Studies and Discipline of Public Schools. By George Moberly, D.C.L., Head Master of Winchester College. *Second Edition.* 8vo. 2s. 6d.

Speech delivered by the Right Hon. B. Disraeli, M.P., at a Public Meeting in aid of the Oxford Diocesan Society for the Augmentation of Small Benefices, held at High Wycombe, October 30th, 1862. Published by permission. 3d., or 2s. 6d. per dozen.

Congregational Music. A Sermon, preached before the Choral Association of the Diocese of Llandaff, in the Cathedral of Llandaff, on Oct. 16, 1862. By Alfred Ollivant, D.D., Bishop of Llandaff. 8vo. 6d.

"The Waiting Isles." A Sermon preached at the Farewell Service of the Mission to the Sandwich Islands, in Westminster Abbey, July 23, 1862. By the Right Rev. the Bishop of Honolulu. 8vo. 1s.

ANGLO-CONTINENTAL SOCIETY.

The BOOKS and TRACTS published by this Society may now be had of Messrs. RIVINGTON.

The ANNUAL PAPER for 1862, containing a Catalogue of the Society's Publications, is now ready.

The REPORT to the Subscribers to the Special Italian Fund is now ready, price 6*d*.

PERIODICALS

PUBLISHED BY

MESSRS. RIVINGTON.

Monthly, price Sixpence,

The COLONIAL CHURCH CHRONICLE, and MISSIONARY JOURNAL.

This Periodical was set on foot more than fifteen years ago, with the object of circulating valuable information which would otherwise be unattainable by the Church at large, and to afford a means of eliciting the opinions of persons engaged or interested in Missionary Work.

It is hoped that this endeavour has not been fruitless. In the volumes already published will be found many valuable communications, with Records of Missionary Labour and Articles on Missionary Subjects of great and permanent interest.

Monthly, at One Penny,

The CHURCH INSTITUTION CIRCULAR.

(*continued.*)

Quarterly, at 3d. per Number,
IN CONNEXION WITH
THE INCORPORATED SOCIETY FOR PROMOTING
THE ENLARGEMENT, BUILDING, AND REPAIRING OF CHURCHES
AND CHAPELS IN ENGLAND AND WALES,

The Church Builder,

AN ILLUSTRATED JOURNAL OF
CHURCH EXTENSION IN ENGLAND AND WALES.
Supplied post-free to all Subscribers of One Shilling and
Fourpence per annum, paid in advance.

The Editor solicits the co-operation of Churchmen in his efforts to render this Periodical subservient to the interests of the Church Building Society, and to the work of Church Extension generally in England and Wales. All Communications should be addressed to the Editor, No. 7, Whitehall, London, S.W.

Nos. I. to V. are published.

Quarterly, at 1d. per Number,
CHURCH-WORK AMONG THE MASSES; in connexion with the London Diocesan Church Building Society.

Nos. I. to VI. are published.

Quarterly, at One Penny,
The HOME MISSION FIELD of the CHURCH of ENGLAND; in connexion with the Additional Curates' Society.

Nos. I. to XVII. are published.

RIVINGTONS, WATERLOO PLACE, LONDON.

PSALMS AND HYMNS

ADAPTED TO THE

SERVICES OF THE CHURCH OF ENGLAND.

BY THE REV. W. J. HALL, M.A.,

late Priest in Ordinary to Her Majesty, and Vicar of Tottenham.

From the great care bestowed upon this collection (under the immediate supervision of the late Lord Bishop of London), that it should be sound in doctrine, spiritual in tone, and practical in tendency, it has been most extensively adopted throughout this country, as well as in our Dependencies and Colonies, in America, and also in most of the English Churches abroad. Nearly a million and a half have been sold altogether of the various Editions.

THIS WORK IS PRINTED IN THE FOLLOWING SIZES :—

	s.	d.
32mo, Nonpareil type, cloth limp, cut flush	0	8
———————— cloth, boards	1	0
———————— sheep	1	2
———————— roan, with gilt edges	1	6
32mo and 48mo, Fine Paper, Pearl type, cloth, gold mitre, g. edges	2	0
———————————————— purple morocco	4	0
24mo, Bourgeois type, cloth limp, cut flush	1	3
———————— cloth, boards	1	6
———————— sheep	1	8
———————— roan, with gilt edges	2	0
24mo, Fine Paper, Bourgeois type, cloth, with gold mitre	2	0
———————————————— purple calf	3	0
———————————————— purple calf, extra, gilt edges	3	6
———————————————— morocco, gilt edges	4	6
18mo, Pica type, cloth, with gold mitre	3	0
———————— roan, with gilt edges, or purple calf	4	0
———————— purple calf, extra, gilt edges	4	6
———————— morocco	5	6
Octavo, Pica type, cloth, with gold mitre	8	0
———————— morocco, gilt edges	12	0

Messrs. RIVINGTON keep several sizes of the Psalms and Hymns, bound with the Book of Common Prayer.

A SELECTION of PSALM and HYMN TUNES, *with Chants, Sanctuses, &c. harmonized for* FOUR VOICES, *and especially adapted to this Work.*

	£	s.	d.
Royal 8vo, cloth	0	12	0
———— half-bound in calf	0	14	0
———— bound in whole calf	0	16	0
———— calf extra, gilt edges	0	18	0
———— purple morocco	1	1	0

Also a HAND-BOOK edition of the above for Congregational use. 3s. 6d.

A Considerable Allowance made to the Clergy, Organists, and for Charitable Purposes.

WORKS
EDITED FOR THE SYNDICS
OF THE
CAMBRIDGE UNIVERSITY PRESS.
SOLD BY RIVINGTONS,
CAMBRIDGE WAREHOUSE, 32, PATERNOSTER ROW,
AND 3, WATERLOO PLACE, LONDON.

Pearson's Exposition of the Creed; edited by Temple Chevallier, B.D., Professor of Mathematics in the University of Durham, and late Fellow and Tutor of St. Catharine's College, Cambridge. Second Edition. 8vo. 10s. 6d.

Select Discourses, by John Smith, late Fellow of Queens' College, Cambridge. Edited by H. G. Williams, B.D., Professor of Arabic in the University. Royal 8vo. 10s. 6d.

The Works of Isaac Barrow, compared with the Original MSS. enlarged with Materials hitherto unpublished. A New Edition, by A. Napier, M.A., of Trinity College, Vicar of Holkham, Norfolk. 9 vols. 8vo. 4l. 14s. 6d.

A Treatise of the Pope's Supremacy, and a Discourse concerning the Unity of the Church. By Isaac Barrow. 8vo. 12s.

Wheatly on the Common Prayer; edited by G. E. Corrie, D.D., Master of Jesus College, Examining Chaplain to the Lord Bishop of Ely. 8vo. 10s. 6d.

The Gospel according to Saint Matthew in Anglo-Saxon and Northumbrian Versions, synoptically arranged: with Collations of the best Manuscripts. By J. M. Kemble, M.A., and Archdeacon Hardwick, late Christian Advocate. 10s.

Cambridge Greek and English Testament, in Parallel Columns on the same page. Edited by J. Scholefield, M.A., late Regius Professor of Greek in the University. Fourth Edition. Small 8vo. 7s. 6d., or 12s. in morocco.

Cambridge Greek Testament. Ex editione Stephani tertia, 1550. Small 8vo. 3s. 6d.

The Homilies, with Various Readings, and the Quotations from the Fathers given at length in the Original Languages. Edited by G. E. Corrie, D.D. 8vo. 10s. 6d.

Archbishop Usher's Answer to a Jesuit, with other Tracts on Popery. Edited by J. Scholefield, M.A. 8vo. 13s. 6d.

Lectures on Divinity delivered in the University of Cambridge. By John Hey, D.D. Third Edition, by T. Turton, D.D., Lord Bishop of Ely. 2 vols. 8vo. 30s.

A complete List of the Publications of the Cambridge University Press may be had on application to Messrs. Rivington.

BIBLES,
COMMON PRAYER BOOKS,
&c.,

PRINTED AT

The Cambridge University Press.

MESSRS. RIVINGTON

BEG LEAVE TO ANNOUNCE THAT THEY HAVE BEEN APPOINTED AGENTS FOR THE SALE OF THE ABOVE EDITIONS,

WHICH MAY BE SEEN AT

No. 3, WATERLOO PLACE, PALL MALL,

AND AT THEIR CAMBRIDGE WAREHOUSE,

No. 32, PATERNOSTER ROW, LONDON.

Catalogues may be had gratis.

GILBERT AND RIVINGTON, PRINTERS, ST. JOHN'S SQUARE, LONDON.

www.ingramcontent.com/pod-product-compliance
Lightning Source LLC
Chambersburg PA
CBHW022113160426
43197CB00009B/1003